"Fr. Mark Scott, OCSO, presents here a series of chapter talks, the fruits of study and reflection on the Gospel of Matthew. Well versed in the scholarly study of the Gospels, his years of reflection on the text result in unexpected insights derived from both biblical and non-biblical perspectives, including the differences between Gospel narratives of the same event."

—Martha Fessler Krieg, lay Cistercian associate and
independent scholar

MONASTIC WISDOM SERIES: NUMBER SIXTY-SEVEN

Loving Jesus

Monastery Talks on the Gospel According to Saint Matthew

Mark A. Scott, OCSO

Cistercian Publications
www.cistercianpublications.org

LITURGICAL PRESS
Collegeville, Minnesota
www.litpress.org

A Cistercian Publications title published by Liturgical Press

Cistercian Publications
Editorial Offices
161 Grosvenor Street
Athens, Ohio 45701
www.cistercianpublications.org

1   2   3   4   5   6   7   8   9

Library of Congress Cataloging-in-Publication Data

Names: Scott, Mark A. (Mark Alexander), 1948- author.
Title: Loving Jesus : monastery talks on the gospel according to Saint Matthew / Mark A. Scott, OCSO.
Description: Collegeville, Minnesota : Cistercian Publications, [2023] | Series: Monastic wisdom series ; no. 67 | Summary: "Originally given as Monastery Talks to his confreres, Mark A. Scott, OCSO, presents these commentaries to ecclesial communities and individual Christians focusing on the 'face' of Jesus provided in chapters four through nine of the Gospel according to Saint Matthew: loving Jesus"— Provided by publisher.
Identifiers: LCCN 2022037616 (print) | LCCN 2022037617 (ebook) | ISBN 9780879070656 (trade paperback) | ISBN 9780879070663 (epub) | ISBN 9780879070663 (pdf) | ISBN 9780879071943 (pdf)
Subjects: LCSH: Bible. Matthew—Commentaries.
Classification: LCC BS2575.53 .S38 2023 (print) | LCC BS2575.53 (ebook) | DDC 226.2/07—dc23/eng/20221130
LC record available at https://lccn.loc.gov/2022037616
LC ebook record available at https://lccn.loc.gov/2022037617

I am pleased to dedicate this book to the honorable monks
of New Melleray Abbey, Peosta, IA, who heard these talks
in their original oral versions and who inspired a lot of them.

If he had not loved his enemies, he could not have had
any friends, just as he would have had no one to love if he had
not loved those who were not.

Saint Bernard, *Sermons on the Song of Songs* 20.2 (CF 4:148)

Contents

Acknowledgments

To Thomas X. Davis, OCSO, abbot *emeritus*, and the monks of New Clairvaux Abbey, Vina, California, I give thanks more than I can express for proposing and supporting my studies at the Pontifical Biblical Institute, Rome. Several people read and commented on this book in its early stages: Dom Paul Mark Schwan, OCSO, and Dom Thomas X. Davis, OCSO, both of New Clairvaux Abbey, Vina; Deacon Charles A. Bobertz; Oliver Coughlin; Sister Katherine Doyle, RSM; Sister Gail Fitzpatrick, OCSO; Linda Harrington; James Koewler; Roger Lipsey; Teresa Mahon; Nick Majesky; Darla Bedford Moe; and Sister Nancy Lee Smith, IHM. To you, thanks for your friendship, encouragement, and honest feedback. As executive editor of Cistercian Publications, Marsha L. Dutton, PhD, has with kindness, tact, persistence, and Christian graciousness rescued the text from many blunders in grammar, logic, and syntax. For much of the clarity the book may have, readers can join me in giving thanks to Dr. Dutton.

Abbreviations

ACCS   *Ancient Christian Commentary on Scripture.* Westmont, IL: InterVarsity Press, 2001.

ACW   Ancient Christian Writers

CC 143   Gregory the Great. *Moralia in Iob.* Corpus Christianorum Series Latina 143. Ed. Marcus Adriaen. Turnholt: Brepols, 1979.

CCC   *Catechism of the Catholic Church*

CF   Cistercian Fathers Series, Cistercian Publications

CF 4   Bernard of Clairvaux. *The Works of Saint Bernard of Clairvaux*, Vol. 2, *On the Song of Songs I.* Trans. Kilian Walsh. CF 4. Spencer, MA: Cistercian Publications, 1971.

CF 7   Bernard of Clairvaux. *The Works of Bernard of Clairvaux*, Vol. 3, *On the Song of Songs II.* Trans. Kilian Walsh. CF 7. Kalamazoo, MI: Cistercian Publications, 1976.

CF 13   Bernard of Clairvaux. *The Works of Bernard of Clairvaux*, Vol. 5, Treatises II. CF 13. Washington, DC: Cistercian Publications, 1974.

CF 54   Bernard of Clairvaux. *Sermons for the Autumn Season.* Trans. Irene Edmonds. CF 54. Collegeville, MN: Cistercian Publications, 2016.

CF 68   Bernard of Clairvaux. *Monastic Sermons*. Trans. Daniel Griggs. CF 68. Collegeville, MN: Cistercian Publications, 2016.

CF 83   Saint Aelred of Rievaulx. *Homilies on the Prophetic Burdens of Isaiah*. Trans. Lewis White. CF 83. Collegeville, MN: Cistercian Publications, 2018.

Coll   *Collectanea Cisterciensia*

Ded   Saint Bernard, Sermons for the Dedication of a Church

Dial   Saint Gregory the Great, *Dialogues*

Did   *Didache*

Dil   Saint Bernard, *On Loving God* (*De diligendo Deo*)

Div   Saint Bernard, *Sermons on Various Things* (*De diversis*)

DV   Dogmatic Constitution on Divine Revelation, *Dei Verbum* (Second Vatican Council)

GE   Pope Francis, *Gaudete et exultate*

LXX   Septuagint (Greek version of the Hebrew Old Testament)

Mart   Saint Bernard, Homily for the Feast of Saint Martin of Tours

Mor in Job   Gregory the Great, *Moralia in Iob*

NABRE   New American Bible, Revised Edition

NMA   New Melleray Abbey, Peosta, IA

OCSO   Cistercian Order of the Strict Observance

Oner   Saint Aelred, Sermons on the Burdens of Isaiah

OS   Saint Bernard, Sermons for the Solemnity of All Saints

RB   Rule of Saint Benedict

SC   Saint Bernard, Sermons on the Song of Songs

SME   *Sancta Mater Ecclesia,* On the Historical Truth of the Gospels (Pontifical Biblical Commission)

Wars   Josephus. *The Wars of the Jews.* In *The Works of Flavius Josephus,* translated by William Whiston. Vol. 1. Grand Rapids, MI: Baker, 1974.

Author's Note

Most of these talks were prepared for my brothers of New Melleray Abbey, Peosta, IA, when I was abbot there (2013–2020). New Melleray is a community of the Roman Catholic Order of Cistercians of the Strict Observance (OCSO), also known as Trappists. Like all monastics of the OCSO, the monks of New Melleray follow the sixth-century Rule of Saint Benedict (RB).[1]

These talks were an attempt to "bring forth both new and old" from what I had learned about the kingdom of God[2] and about Scripture, as Saint Benedict, following Jesus, says that an abbot should do (RB 64.9; Matt 13:52). They are "monastery" talks. They were delivered by a monk to monks in an exclusively monastic context. They reflect a monastic way of reading and thinking. But because monks are thoroughly human, I know that people with other backgrounds will easily translate to their own circumstances what is offered here. As "talks," they retain in their printed form something of their original oral tone.

The talks are on chapters four through nine of the gospel according to Saint Matthew. The gospel unit Matthew 4:12–9:35 seems to be Matthew's introduction of Jesus, Son of David (Matt 1:1) and

---

1. For New Melleray Abbey see https://newmelleray.org/; for the Order of Cistercians of the Strict Observance see https://ocso.org/; for Saint Benedict's Rule for Monasteries see http://archive.osb.org/rb/.

2. The phrase "kingdom of [the] heavens" is used in Matthew's gospel thirty-one times, the phrase "kingdom of God" four times, and the phrase "kingdom of [my, your, their] Father" four times. The three phrases refer to the same reality. It would be worth it to ask the reason for using three similar but different phrases to talk about the same thing, but it is a question that I will set aside in these talks.

Beloved Son of the one Jesus would call Father (Matt 3:17; 26:39); because Matthew is the first thing to greet someone opening the New Testament, it is also the New Testament's introduction to Jesus. The teachings and stories in chapters four through nine are framed by notices that Jesus taught in synagogues, proclaimed the Good News, and healed (Matt 4:23; 9:35). In chapter 4:12-22 Matthew gives the biblical basis for Jesus' ministry and narrates the call of the first four disciples who will thereafter accompany Jesus. The talks follow the order of Matthew's gospel. Just as the gospel yields its ripe fruit when you read it straight through rather than skipping around, so too with the talks. Nevertheless, each talk pretty much stands on its own so that you do not need to read the talks in the order given here. The talks are numbered. When a particular talk refers to something in another one, I have supplied the number of that other talk.

Scripture quotations are generally from the New American Bible Revised Edition (NABRE); in many cases, though, I have given my own translation or modified the NABRE.

As for methodology, I find it in what Gregory the Great says about his approach to the book of Job: *in hoc opera spiritali intellectui deseruire*, "I minister to the spiritual understanding," knowing, though, that "the spiritual fruit" is produced from the root of the truth [of language and] of history (*ex radice historiae ueritas producit*) (Mor in Job 6.2; CC 143:285). In my reading of the gospel I have been influenced by the historical approach of N. T. Wright and by the philological approach of the Pontifical Biblical Institute, Rome, as represented by, for instance, Clemens Stock, SJ.

When I delivered these talks at New Melleray I had not read Eleonore Stump. When I was putting them together for this book, though, I had already read Stump's *Atonement* and was reading her *Wandering in Darkness: Narrative and the Problem of Suffering*. Time and again I discovered in the latter book elucidations of things I had said in the talks.

M. A. S.

Preface: Reading the Gospel

A tip about getting to know Jesus from the gospels: when the four canonical gospels, those New Testament texts commonly attributed to Saint Matthew, Saint Mark, Saint Luke, and Saint John, give more than one account of something in the life of Jesus, read all of them and not just one. We need to consider all of them together as well as each of them on its own, to get the truest picture of Jesus we can.

The Dogmatic Constitution on Divine Revelation, *Dei Verbum* (DV), of the Second Vatican Council (1965), says that the gospels present four faces of the same Jesus, while always telling us "the authentic truth" about him (DV 19).

Just a year before that conciliar document came out, the Pontifical Biblical Commission published its own document, *Sancta Mater Ecclesia* (SME), "On the Historical Truth of the Gospels" (1964). SME influenced DV in a powerful way.[1]

SME says that the evangelists, "each using an approach suited to his specific purpose," recorded the events of the Gospel for the benefit of the churches (SME 13). They "selected those items most suited to their specific purpose" and "reported Christ's deeds and words in varying contexts, choosing whichever one would be of greatest help to the reader in trying to understand a particular utterance" (SME 15, 16).

1. See James Chukwuma Okoye, *Scripture in the Church: The Synod on the Word of God* (Collegeville, MN: Liturgical Press, 2011), 72.

Vatican Council II's *Dei Verbum* affirms that the fourfold Gospel has from the earliest times been the canonical inspired Word of God for the Church: "Under the inspiration of the Holy Spirit" the evangelists "handed on to us in writing the same message" that the apostles had preached: "the foundation of our faith: the fourfold gospel, according to Matthew, Mark, Luke and John" (DV 18).

The four gospels, says *Dei Verbum*, "faithfully hand on what Jesus, the Son of God, while he lived among men, really did and taught for their eternal salvation" (DV 19).

Let's try an experiment. Jesus goes to Galilee after his temptations in the desert (see talk #1). Each of the synoptic evangelists, Mark, Matthew, and Luke, tells the story in his own way (John is silent on both the temptations and the move to Galilee).

Mark says, "After John had been handed-over[2] Jesus went into Galilee" (Mark 1:14). Matthew says, "Hearing then that John had been handed-over he withdrew into Galilee" (Matt 4:12). Luke says, "And Jesus returned in the power of the Spirit into Galilee" (Luke 4:14).

Both Mark and Matthew connect the return to Galilee with the arrest (handing-over) of John. This link with John's arrest is unexpected. It comes out of the blue. Neither Matthew nor Mark has said anything yet about John being arrested. In those gospels we just met John, and he was at work preaching and baptizing (Mark 1:2-11; Matt 3:1-17).

But now in Matthew and Mark Jesus' move to Galilee is under the shadow of the arrest of John. Why was he arrested? Where is he? What does his arrest mean to Jesus, and what does it have to do with his return to Galilee? Mark and Matthew give us no clues at this point in their accounts.

For his part, Luke says nothing at all about John in connection with Jesus' return to Galilee, even though Luke alone of the three

---

2. In the Greek, this is one word, so I hyphenate the two English words when they are in the context of a biblical quotation.

has already told us, even before his notice of the baptism of Jesus, about the arrest of John (Luke 3:18-20). Only much later in their respective accounts will Mark and Matthew tell us about John's arrest, and when they do, it will be a flashback, for John will already have been killed. And whereas Luke says nothing about the actual death of John, Mark and Matthew will each give an unforgettable picture of it (Mark 6:14-29; Matt 14:1-12).

So that is one thing we can notice, that for Mark and Matthew Jesus' movement is under the shadow of John, even his early movement from Judea to Galilee after the baptism and temptations. For Matthew and Mark, Jesus' public career starts from the arrest of John, leaving unexplained, though, why Jesus stayed in Judea until John's arrest, and leaving us to figure out why the arrest should have had any particular and decisive significance for Jesus.

For Luke, the motivation for Jesus' return to Galilee has nothing to do with John. Something else is going on, someone else is motivating Jesus, and Luke makes clear who it is: "And Jesus *returned in* the power of *the Spirit* into Galilee" (Luke 4:14). For the third evangelist, rather than Jesus' seeing the implications for himself of the handing over of John, it is the power of the Spirit that moves Jesus, just as it was in Luke's account of Jesus going to the desert of temptations: "Full of the Holy Spirit, he *returned* from the Jordan and was led, *in the Spirit*, into the desert" (Luke 4:1).

So we have in the gospels three accounts of Jesus' return to Galilee after his baptism and temptations. The event is the same, but it is told in three ways that differ from each other.

A generally accepted story of how we arrived at the written canonical gospels is that first there was an oral tradition about Jesus, including liturgical preaching. That oral tradition was written down and edited to finally result in the canonical gospels. As Ben Meyer explains, "From the only point of view coherent with the faith-consciousness of primitive Christianity, there follows . . . the primacy for faith of the New Testament scriptures themselves over a narrowly conceived" attempt to nail down "what really happened."[3]

I am going to use Eleonore Stump here about a perceived problem with having more than one canonical account of Jesus, and a solution to that problem, because I think she says it very well. The problem is that sometimes there is "considerable variation" between or among the accounts, and such variation can result in real tensions and apparent contradictions.

The solution that patristic and medieval interpreters came up with is what we call "harmonies." Those early interpreters, Stump explains, "agreed in supposing that all four gospel texts could and should be combined into one larger narrative; and they supposed that that larger narrative is told only in part, and only from one point of view, by any one gospel. . . . They took everything in all the gospels to be true; and then they tried to find a way" to put everything together to form a consistent narrative, a harmony.[4]

The gospels, says DV, give us "the authentic truth about Jesus" "under the inspiration of the Holy Spirit" (DV 19, 11), and that truth is in sharpest focus when we consider it from every point of view available to us.

Each of the four gospel portraits of Jesus is a good portrait. Each stands on its own. At the same time, because the four portraits are from different angles and in different light, it is worth looking at them all. In these Monastery Talks I focus on the "face" of Jesus provided by the gospel according to Saint Matthew: loving Jesus. There follows, then, something for the readers of this little book to do to complete what I have begun. If one or more of the other gospels tells the same or a similar thing, I give chapter and

3. See Ben F. Meyer, *The Aims of Jesus* (London: SCM, 1979), 74.

4. Eleonore Stump, *Wandering in Darkness: Narrative and the Problem of Suffering* (Oxford: Clarendon, 2010), 312–13. By pointing to medieval harmonies, I am not endorsing the creation and use of gospel harmonies. Better for today's reader are synopses, for instance, Kurt Aland, *Synopsis of the Four Gospels* (Minneapolis: Fortress, 1985).

verse references to those accounts at the head of my treatment of Matthew's version, and it will be up to the readers to look at those other accounts.

Mark A. Scott, OCSO, SSL
January 6, 2022
Solemnity of the Epiphany of the Lord

Monastery Talks

1

On Matthew 4:12-13

(Mark 1:14-15; Luke 4:14-15)

Sometime after Jesus' baptism and temptations in the desert, John the Baptist was handed over. Both Matthew and Mark say so.

Both evangelists use the verb "handed-over."[1] John was handed over. John is the passive subject of the verb, so even grammatically John undergoes a passion; he suffers something at the hands of someone else.

If someone says that John was handed over they are inviting us to ask, by whom? The answer is simple: by God, the only agent in the Bible who really matters. When you read the gospels you can be 99.9% certain that the real subject of a passive verb is God.

John is handed over. John is so totally an instrument of God that even when it comes to his being handed over to Herod no one is allowed to do it but God. Later Jesus will say the same thing about himself: "The Son of Man is about to be handed-over . . . and on the third day he will be raised" (Matt 17:22, 23). We ask, "By whom will he be handed over?" and we know the answer, and we also know the answer to the question, "By whom will he be raised?"

This is not just a manner of speaking. It has the weight of a Credo. It is the original, solemn, and enduring Christian faith. See Saint Paul's letter to the Romans, written before either Mark

1. See Preface, n. 2.

or Matthew wrote his gospel: "Righteousness," says Paul, "is to be reckoned to us who *believe* in the one who *raised* Jesus our Lord from the dead, [Jesus] who *was handed-over* for our trespasses and *was raised* for our justification" (Rom 4:24-25), and we understand, *handed over by God* and *raised by God*. This is the Christian faith, and the Christian God.

Both Mark and Matthew link Jesus' return to Galilee with John's being handed over. The link is strong in Matthew but weak in Mark.

Mark says, "Now after John was handed-over, Jesus came into Galilee" (Mark 1:14). If there is a link, it is not a causal link but merely a temporal one. Mark simply locates Jesus' move to Galilee in relation to the time of John's being handed over.

Matthew is quite different: "Now hearing that John had been handed-over, he withdrew into Galilee" (Matt 4:12). Mark is not interested in whether Jesus knew about John's arrest. Matthew, though, puts Jesus' knowing of it in the foreground. In Matthew, the real connection between John's being handed over and Jesus' move to Galilee is in Jesus' own psychology: "Now hearing." It is Jesus' hearing that motivates the move.

We know that in the Bible hearing is more than just a physical sensation. "Hear, O Israel!" "This is my Son, my beloved; hear him," "The sheep hear his voice" (Deut 6:4; Matt 17:5; John 10:3). Saint Benedict conveys the full meaning of biblical hearing in the Prologue to his Rule: "Listen my son, receive, and bring to completion" (RB Prol. 1). To hear is at once physical, noetic, and moral; hearing includes both understanding and effective response to what is understood. So, hearing is *obedience* in the monastic sense of that term.

"Now hearing that John had been handed-over," Jesus saw the hand of God at work in John's fate and understood that that same hand rested on him. "It is probable," says Ben F. Meyer, "owing to the nexus between 'prophet' and 'violent fate' in contemporary religious tradition (cf. Luke 13.33), that the prospect of a violent death belonged . . . to [Jesus'] self-understanding from the start."

John's arrest, and especially his eventual execution by Herod, brought that prospect very close to home.[2]

And so Jesus went home to Galilee. Before he would do the martyr's work in Jerusalem, he would do the prophet's work in Galilee—assemble disciples, teach them, and proclaim a prophet's interpretation of the past, a prophet's indictment of the present, and a prophet's vision of the future.

"Now hearing that John had been handed-over, he withdrew into Galilee." That sentence in chapter four of Matthew reminds us of another in chapter fourteen (for in the world of Scripture you can remember things before they happen; that is why Christians have such a hard time in the secular culture; their timing is off). In chapter fourteen Matthew writes, "Now hearing, Jesus withdrew from there in a boat to a desert place by himself" (Matt 14:13).

We have the same pattern here as in chapter four. Jesus hears something and as a consequence withdraws. In chapter four we know what Jesus heard, that John had been handed over. The verse from chapter fourteen doesn't say what Jesus heard, so we have to look for it.

Earlier in chapter fourteen Matthew told the story of Herod's bizarre birthday party with the guests, the dancing girl, and Herodias's intrigue that resulted in the death of John, concluding with, "And John's disciples came and took the body and buried it; and they went and told Jesus" (Matt 14:12).

Then it says, "Now hearing, Jesus withdrew" (Matt 14:13).

So is the story of the death of John that John's disciples told Jesus right after they buried John's body what Jesus heard? But with respect to Matthew's developing narrative about Jesus, the account of John's death that Matthew just related is a flashback; with respect to Jesus' present in Matthew's story, John's death was not contemporaneous but in the indeterminate past.

2. Ben F. Meyer, *The Aims of Jesus* (London: SCM, 1979), 122, 252.

If, then, we say that what Jesus "heard" at this point in his life was the story of John's death, and hearing that he withdrew to a desert place, then the rest of Matthew's story about Jesus, including Jesus' passion and death, would all be part of the same flashback. All the rest of the gospel story would have its starting point not with Jesus' narrative present but with the death of John in the indeterminate past.

This time warp would create all kinds of narrative problems for the reader, and even theological ones; Matthew is too good a writer and a theologian to make a mistake like that.

So what *did* Jesus hear in chapter fourteen that moved him to withdraw? Listen to what Matthew recounts at the *beginning* of chapter fourteen. It takes place in Jesus' present: "At that time, Herod the tetrarch heard about the fame of Jesus; and he said to his servants, 'This is John the Baptist, he has been raised from the dead; that is why these powers are at work in him'" (Matt 14:1-2). Then Matthew tells the story of the death of John and the disciples burying the body and going to tell Jesus, all as a flashback.

Then, returning to Jesus' present, Matthew says, "Now, when Jesus heard, he withdrew."

What Jesus heard, then, was that Herod the tetrarch, who Jesus knew had put John to death in the past—because John's disciples had told him—had now in Jesus' present heard of Jesus' fame and was thinking that Jesus was John raised from the dead.

What moved Jesus to withdraw to a desert place was Jesus' hearing of Herod's hearing of him now, in Jesus' present (Matt 14:13, 1). Herod, who had killed John in the past, now had his attention on Jesus in the present, and that fact had consequences for Jesus' future. So, as Jesus had done in chapter four after hearing that John had been arrested, at 14:13 he again withdrew.

Matthew says, "Jesus *withdrew* into Galilee" (Matt 4:12). What do you want to say when you use the word *withdraw*?

Although Matthew says, "withdrew *to*," the word *withdraw* implies a starting point as well as a destination. A withdrawal *to* is also a withdrawing *from*, and you withdraw *from* a place or a situation because you sense that there is a threat of some kind that you want to get away from.

If you read the gospel of Matthew from the beginning, when you come to 4:12 you will already have encountered withdrawal twice. The Magi, "warned in a dream not to return to Herod, *withdrew* by another way to their own country" (Matt 2:12), and Joseph, "hearing that Archelaus" had replaced his father Herod as king and "warned in a dream, *withdrew* to the district of Galilee" (Matt 2:22).

So while Matthew says that Jesus "withdrew to Galilee," we have a subliminal sense that Jesus is also withdrawing *from*, and not just from a place, but also from something threatening *in* that place. We know what that threat is: it is the threat contained in the fact of John's having been handed over to—having been arrested by—Herod, the threat of the fate of a prophet of Israel now rolling quietly toward Jesus.

And finally there is the word itself, *withdraw*. In Greek it is *anachoreo*. The noun is *anachoresis*, the state of withdrawal, and from it we get the English word *anchorite*.

A core monastic and Cistercian practice is what we call "separation from the world" (see Constitutions OCSO 29). "Separation from the world" is the ancient monastic ascesis of *anachoresis*, withdrawal. It is a practice that must always have its starting point in the gospel and in Jesus' own *anachoresis* in the face of a mortal threat, and as a way of best using the terrestrial time available to him for fulfilling his work as both prophet and martyr.

> O, that I had wings like a dove to fly away and be at rest.
> *But it was a dove that rested on you.*

2

On Matthew 4:13, 16

(Mark 1:14; Luke 4:14, 16–29;
see Luke 1:79)

"When he heard that John had been handed-over, Jesus withdrew into Galilee" (Matt 4:12).

> If it were an enemy that had done this, I could hide from him. *Even if you went to hell, you'd find me there.*

Jesus understood that it was God who had handed John over, the same God who had said of Jesus, "My son, with whom I am well pleased" (Matt 3:17).

But could it be the same God? What kind of God, what kind of Father, was he? Jesus withdrew into Galilee as if withdrawing from a fate, but "Where can I go from your spirit, or where can I flee from your face? If I climb the heavens, if I lie in the grave, you are there" (Ps 139:7, 8).

"He withdrew into Galilee, and abandoning Nazareth he went and made his home in Capernaum by the sea" (Matt 4:12b, 13a).

Entering the region of Galilee, Jesus apparently first went to Nazareth, his hometown. To see his parents and his family? Matthew gives us no information. It is at this point, though, that Luke, alone of the evangelists, gives the account of Jesus standing to read in the synagogue of Nazareth and proclaiming when he'd finished, "today this scripture has been fulfilled in your hearing" (Luke 4:16-21). The entire incident concludes with the people of Nazareth taking Jesus out of town to throw him over a cliff (Luke 4:29).

Matthew is silent about this hostility toward Jesus in his hometown. He only hints at it with the word *abandon*. Jesus abandoned Nazareth, Matthew says, and we get the idea that something unpleasant had compelled this definitive break with his hometown.

Did Jesus do a *geographical*?

To do a geographical is to attempt to solve a conflict by leaving the place of the conflict and going somewhere else. Usually conflicts have to do with other people. So the idea of a geographical is that if you leave where those other people are and go somewhere else then you resolve the conflict. Did Jesus do that when he abandoned Nazareth and went to Capernaum?

But often, doing a geographical does not work out the way we think it will. That is because if a conflict has to do with another person or some other people, they are only part of the story. The conflict also has to do with us, so if we do a geographical and leave the other person, we still haven't left ourselves.

You can be sure that sooner or later whatever conflict we thought we were leaving will materialize in the new place we have moved to, because we ourselves are one party to the conflict. In the new situation we will without fail find someone else to take the other person's place in it.

Monks have a really difficult time doing geographicals because of our vow of stability. I have often wondered if my own history in that regard is not really a history of doing geographicals.[1] But for most monks, there is no place to go, except to a different choir stall. Or you can take the west cloister instead of the east cloister to get to church, or you can withdraw from a brother through an unholy silence. Avoidance can be a geographical in a monastic setting, and avoidance can easily turn into a habit of passive aggression. It's nasty.

---

1. Going to New Melleray was the sixth significant change of place after I entered monastic life just a little over thirty years before.

Saint Benedict as usual has some good advice. He doesn't want the good vow of stability to be a den of bitterness. So he says, as a general principle, "Rid your heart of all deceit," and then, "If you have a dispute with someone, make peace with him before the sun goes down" (RB 4.24, 73). This advice is for cenobites who persevere in the battle line of the ranks of the brothers (see RB 1.5).

That one word *abandoned* invites me to imagine a whole unspoken world of emotions on Jesus' part and on the part of those left behind. The memories. The goodbyes, if there were goodbyes. Joseph—his father, so it was thought—the carpenter. His brothers and sisters and friends. The people he would have built things and repaired things for. Hiking with friends, eating, drinking, and singing together. Religious holidays: the lights and the political undertones of Hanukkah, the solemn joy of Yom Kippur, the fun of Sukkot. The trips with Joseph to Sepphoris, the special love for Mary his mother, and hers for him. Her fragrance, her quirky, ironic sense of humor that he inherited.

> To my own kin I have become an outcast, a stranger to the children of my mother.

Why?

> Here I am in anguish. I looked for solace, but there was none, for consolers, not one could I find.

Why? What happened? What prompted Jesus to abandon his hometown and settle in Capernaum? Matthew does not tell us because his concern is elsewhere. As he will present it, whatever Jesus' motivation was for abandoning Nazareth, God found the move an occasion for bringing into history something God had promised through his prophets long ago.

There was some compensation for any pain involved in abandoning Nazareth for Capernaum. The first-century historian Josephus writes about the sheer natural beauty and fertility of the region around the Sea of Galilee where Capernaum was: "Its soil is so fruitful," for instance, "that all sorts of trees can grow upon it, . . . particularly walnuts, . . . palm trees, . . . fig trees . . . and olives." Josephus observes that the environment there "forces those plants that are naturally enemies to one another to agree together. . . . And besides the good temperature of the air, it is also watered from a most fertile fountain" (Wars 3.10.8).

And then there was the Sea itself, with its abundance and variety of fish.

Here is Matthew's version of what God had said through the prophet and what he was now fulfilling in Jesus of Nazareth come to Capernaum:

> *Land of Zebulun and land of Naphtali,*
> *the way to the sea, beyond the Jordan,*
> *Galilee of the Gentiles,*
> *the people who sit in darkness have seen a great light,*
> *on those dwelling in a land overshadowed by death light has*
> *arisen.* (see Matt 4:16; Isa 8:23–9:1; see also Isa 58:10)

This is not the first time that Matthew steps out from behind his narrative to speak to his readers (see, for instance, Matthew 1:22-23 on the birth of Jesus and the prophecy about the virgin), and it won't be the last (see, for instance, Matthew 8:17, on the Servant bearing our diseases). True, he speaks from behind the veil of prophets' words, but now those words are his own. Those words were telling in hope and expectation the same story whose fulfillment Matthew is telling with his gospel narrative. The gospel writer knows what Jesus is about, what Jesus means. How does he know this? (The question intends what we mean by *inspiration*.[2])

---

2. Take this poem by Kathleen Raine:
>   Never for the first time
>   Love's meeting:
>   We know that we have known for ever
>   Each the other
>   Whose living eyes bring greeting
>   From the long forgotten.

As he does here and in other places, Matthew can step out of his story to tell us what he knows in terms of prophecy fulfillment; then he steps back behind the narrative he has given us and stays mostly out of sight.

Matthew says that Jesus settled in Capernaum by the sea so that as a result what had been said through the prophet Isaiah might be fulfilled.

That is, noting the passive voice, that God might fulfill what God had said through the prophet Isaiah (Matt 4:14). You might even say that God was *behind* Jesus' abandoning Nazareth and moving to Capernaum for God's very purpose, for the purpose of fulfilling what God had said nearly a thousand years earlier.

In any case, Matthew does not give us grounds for thinking that one day while still in Nazareth Jesus heard that passage from Isaiah and said, "That's it! I am going to leave home and settle in Capernaum so that this prophecy will be fulfilled." To think that would be to apply to Jesus a hubris that was foreign to him. It was

---

> Love the centre
> Of a so great embrace,
> Everywhere is here,
> All time, all being
> New in perpetual beginning,
> Old as the stars.

(Kathleen Raine, "A Love Remembered," *The Collected Poems* [Washington, DC: Counterpoint, 2001], 248. Used by permission of Faber and Faber Limited).

What provoked the poet to write this? Someone entered her life, and from the encounter, this poem emerged. Kathleen Raine is the author; there is no doubt. But also, that other as the direct cause of the experience is no less the author, even without writing a word. Maybe that other had had an eye on Raine for a long time. Let's suppose that he got a haircut and then staged a little set-up that would assure his meeting her. Let's suppose, further, that he had the power to provoke from her a happy reaction to the encounter. The attraction, the set-up, the encounter, the provocation, even the haircut: all together is what we mean by inspiration.

not Jesus who was going to fulfill that holy prophecy; it was God, who had spoken it, who would do it.

It was more like this: God saw Jesus settle in Capernaum and said, "Well, look. Now I am fulfilling what I said through the prophet Isaiah."

That is not to say that God's timing is contingent on our own timing and the personal motives for our actions, but it's not to say it isn't, either.

It *is* to say, taking this biblical passage as an example, that a Word of God might be the intimate companion of even our most insignificant actions, and that actions of ours that do not arise from any deliberate intention of *ours* to do God's will in any specific way but are motivated by purely personal, even selfish, reasons, *can* be the *occasions* for God to fulfill his Word.[3]

Take Saint Paul. God had set him apart before he was born, had called him through his grace (Gal 1:15), but it was when the adult Paul was on the way to Damascus breathing threats, intent on a violent destruction of the church, that God brought that divine call out into the open to fulfillment: "he is a chosen vessel of mine" (Gal 1:16; Acts 9:1-29, 15).

3. See, for instance, Mor in Job 6.XVIII.28–33, where Gregory the Great gives several examples of people ending up doing God's will in their very intention to oppose it. Consider the distinction between God's antecedent will and God's consequent will. Eleonore Stump says, "God's antecedent will is what God would have willed if everything in the world had been up to him alone. God's consequent will is what God actually does will, given what God's creatures will." What God "wills in his consequent will, what is the best in the circumstances, might only be the lesser of evils, of the intrinsically good" (Eleonore Stump, *Wandering in Darkness: Narrative and the Problem of Suffering* [Oxford: Clarendon, 2010], 385, 428). Stump derives this distinction from Thomas Aquinas. Gregory explains, "In a marvelous way it happens that what is done without God's willing it is not contrary to God's will when good use is made of evil deeds and those things done in opposition to his designs end up serving them" (Gregory the Great, Mor in Job 6.XVIII.33).

We would like to know, or I would, what Jesus' house was like in Capernaum. Did he rent or buy? And how did he support himself, this inland artisan transplanted to a fishing culture? Did he ever look back? Did he know anyone?

Matthew does not think we need to know these things. He tells us only that God fulfilled his word when Jesus went to Capernaum.

3

On Matthew 4:17

(Mark 1:15)

"Land of Zebulun and land of Naphtali, the way to the sea, beyond the Jordan, Galilee of the Gentiles, the people who sit in darkness have seen a great light, on those dwelling in a land overshadowed by death light has arisen" (see Matt 4:16; Isa 8:23—9:1; see Isa 58:10). That is Matthew's version of God's word through the prophet Isaiah that Matthew says God fulfilled as a result of Jesus' settling in Capernaum (Matt 4:13; #2).

Hearing that John had been handed over, Jesus had withdrawn into Galilee. First he went to Nazareth, his hometown, and then, abandoning Nazareth, he withdrew further into Galilee, settling at Capernaum on the northern shore of the Sea of Galilee (#1, #2).

The perspective of the prophecy from Isaiah is that of the rising sun, from the other side of the Jordan looking west, toward Capernaum, toward Galilee and the land of Zebulun and Naphtali.

In the Song of Deborah, "Zebulun was a people who defied death, Naphtali, too" (Judg 5:18). Yet, as the Second Book of Kings records, in the eighth century, "In the days of Pekah, king of Israel," the king of Assyria—to the east of Israel—came and took Galilee, including Zebulun and "all the land of Naphtali—deporting the inhabitants to Assyria" (2 Kgs 15:29).

By the time Jesus moved to Capernaum, the Assyrian exile had ended long before, but the effects of the exile and its memory were as solid and immovable as the Horns of Hattin. It was still a land of "people sitting in darkness" and "in the region and the shadow of death."

"A light has risen." Matthew doesn't say outright that Jesus *was* that light, that rising sun, but the association he makes is pretty strong, and John the Baptist had said that the "one coming after" him would be an "unquenchable fire" (Matt 3:11, 12).

The sun rises in the east, but Jesus came to Capernaum from Nazareth. Nazareth lies to the west and south of Capernaum, not to the east. And far from any sun expected to arise from Nazareth, as Nathaniel asks in John, "Can *any*thing good be from Nazareth?" (John 1:46).

At least Nathaniel had heard of Nazareth. On the one hand, we know from archeological evidence that the area had been inhabited from as long ago as two thousand years before Jesus. On the other hand, though, outside the twelve times that the name of the village occurs in the New Testament (eleven in the gospels, one in Acts) there is no mention of Nazareth in any known pre-Christian texts.

Contrast the anonymity of Jesus' Nazareth with the renown of Paul's Tarsus, which was said to have surpassed both Athens and Alexandria for its philosophical and political importance. At the time of Jesus, Nazareth had fewer than a thousand people. Anyone coming from Nazareth would have been a nobody. Not "anything good."

To Capernaum from Nazareth Jesus would have brought no formal education, since Nazareth had no schools.[1]

Instead, he brought the Psalms, the Torah, and the Prophets, in Hebrew and in his native Aramaic.

---

1. On the question of Nazareth as Jesus' hometown and of his educational possibilities, see the suggestive remarks by Margaret Hebblethwaite, "The Mary Enigma," *The Tablet* (19/26 December 2020): 12–13. Hebblethwaite's theory is that Mary was not from backwater Nazareth but from cultured Judea (Jerusalem), where she would have been educated and so in a good position to be Jesus' primary educator.

"Rising from the darkness, he is a light for the upright, generous, merciful, and just" (Ps 112:4). For Matthew—no, for God—this Jesus coming to Capernaum from Nazareth in the southwest of Galilee is a light, a rising sun, in perfect disguise. He does not come from outside the land of Zebulun and Naphtali, but from deep within it: Nazareth is in Zebulun and Capernaum in Naphtali. Matthew is saying in his own way what John will later say in his, that Jesus is the Word made Flesh, the light that shines in the darkness, a "bridegroom coming from his tent" to "his own home" (John 1:14, 5, 11; Ps 19:6). But "men loved darkness rather than light" (John 3:19).

In that prophecy from Isaiah there are land and sea, earth and heaven, Gentiles and Israelite tribes, sitting and rising, darkness and vision, death and light of life. We heard what the Jewish historian Josephus had said, that the conditions around the Sea of Galilee forced plants that are naturally enemies to one another to agree together (#2). The rising sun is impartial in the distribution of its gifts of warmth and light. Its gaze encourages the display and the play of the intrinsic harmony of apparent opposites.

And so Jesus of Nazareth comes to Capernaum, makes his home there, and then, at that time, starts the *kerygma*, the proclamation of the Gospel. His words are the first rays of the rising sun: "Repent, for the kingdom of heaven is at hand" (Matt 4:17).

The first rays of the sun do dispel the darkness of the night.

But they also create darkness when they strike the east side of buildings and trees—shadows of immense length and grotesque shapes then inhabit the land, not to mention your own shadow as you stand there vulnerable, in an open place now lit up.

The *kerygma*, the Gospel, the Law of the Lord: Repent. "Nothing is concealed from its burning heat" (Ps 19:7). Even the grotesque features of the heart and soul of those who hear are exposed.

Jesus did not say only "Repent"; he added the reason for repenting: "for the kingdom of heaven is at hand." That addition of the motive is crucial. Simply to tell someone to repent is too vague because there are many kinds of repentance. By stating the motive you make clear what kind of repentance you're talking about.

If you're an eloquent gang member you could say, "Repent, the cops are coming," and you mean, stop beating on that guy and run. Or if you live in a Christian village in the Middle East you might urge neighbors at a village meeting, "Repent, for the jihadists are coming," and you mean, change your religion or you're dead. In the late Middle Ages, you might have said, "Repent, for the Inquisition is coming," or today, "the ACLU is coming," and you mean, change your narrative, at least till the threat passes.

So what kind of repentance do you mean when you say, "Repent, for the kingdom of heaven is at hand"?

You don't use the word *kingdom* to talk about morality, religion, or ideological agendas. *Kingdom* is a social, political word. It is about citizenship, about allegiance, about participation in a commonwealth, about loyalty to a people and to one particular leader and not to another.

So when you say, "Repent, for the kingdom of heaven is at hand," you are calling people to change their citizenship, to shift their allegiance, to stop trusting in that regime and to start trusting in this one, and to be responsible for the choice.

Jesus is calling people to a radical change both in their politics and of the people with whom they wholeheartedly identify. Later, he will make this point in other words: Caesar—or God; mother, father, spouse, and children—or me; those invited but who refuse to come—or the poor, the maimed the lame, the blind (Matt 22:17; 10:37; 22:9 [Luke 15:21]). You cannot serve two masters (Matt 6:24). So, "Repent, for the kingdom of heaven is at hand." The critical time is now.

Saint Paul told the Philippians, "Our citizenship is in heaven" (Phil 3:20). I believe that Saint Benedict had in mind Jesus' *kerygma* and Paul's application of it when he invited the new monk to make a vow of *conversatio morum*. The Latin version of Paul's declaration is "*Nostra . . . conversatio in cælis est.*" *Conversatio* translates the Greek word meaning citizenship. A citizen enjoys rights and assumes obligations. Monastic *conversatio* is not just a moral and intellectual conversion; it is choosing to live holistically as a citizen of the kingdom of heaven. "And from that day" when he promises *conversatio morum suorum*, the newly professed monk "is counted one of the community" (RB 58.23).

The monastery is not heaven, but it is a heavenly, Godly, community. The monastery is a polity, a commonwealth, a *koinonia*. The monk chooses service to the true King by choosing to live under a Rule and an abbot (RB 1.1).

A position like that can put you in all kinds of danger. I mean, what are the kings and Caesars of the time going to say, the kings of Assyria under whatever other name, let alone those other forces Paul talks about, "every principality, authority, power, and dominion" under sentence to be destroyed by the reign of God and of his Christ (Eph 1:22; see 1 Cor 15:25)?

The monastery is not the kingdom of God, but it is governed by the constitution of the kingdom that you find in Jesus' Sermon on the Mount in chapter five of Matthew's gospel, especially the Beatitudes, and in chapter twenty-five of the same text, which ends with, "Whatever you did to the least of my brothers and sisters you did to me," so, "Come, inherit the kingdom prepared for you" (Matt 25:40, 34).

From that time, Jesus began to proclaim, "Repent, for the kingdom of heaven is at hand," and he has never stopped.

4

On Matthew 4:18

(Mark 1:16; Luke 5:1-11;
see John 1:35-42)

"As he walked by the Sea of Galilee he saw two brothers, Simon called Peter and Andrew his brother" (Matt 4:18). Matthew is talking about Jesus. Jesus, come from Nazareth, is now living in Capernaum by the Sea (#2).

The name makes me think of quaint places on the coast of my native California—Carmel-by-the-Sea, Seacliff, Seabright, Half Moon Bay—places of retreat for the wealthy, and of lazy days and easy camaraderie for vagabonds, with coffee shops and good surfing.

Jesus was raised an inlander and is now living in a fishing culture. He was not one of the wealthy, but neither was he exactly a vagabond. He was a preacher, and he was preaching, "Repent, for the kingdom of heaven is at hand" (Matt 4:17; #3). He was a peripatetic preacher; that is, as Aristotle used to do, he preached as he walked, walked as he preached.

Matthew presents Jesus walking by the Sea of Galilee. He considered the Sea of Galilee as he walked by it. It was some thirteen miles long and eight miles wide, an enormous body of water for this small land of Palestine.

At seven hundred feet below sea level, the Sea of Galilee was the lowest freshwater lake on earth. We don't know what this fact of topography might have meant to Jesus; I imagine, though, that he would have loved it.

Jesus knew that not too long before, just forty days and forty nights, he had been baptized in the Jordan River, which ran directly south from the Sea (see Matt 3:13–4:2). He considered that the River Jordan flowed south through the Great Rift Valley, having taken its rise from this very Sea to the north. It was in water coming from here in Galilee that there in the desert of Judea he, anonymous among countless anonymous others, had been baptized by John.

Walking along the Sea, Jesus was at the terrestrial source of something very personal to him, for he would never have been able to forget how there, then, coming up from the waters of the Jordan that were the waters of the Sea under John's hand, "the heavens were opened and he saw the Spirit of God descending like a dove and alighting on him," and especially "a voice from heaven, saying"—really, announcing—"This is my beloved Son, with whom I am well pleased" (Matt 3:16-17).

We know that Jesus walking by the Sea is God-with-us, Emmanuel (Matt 1:23). We know that he was conceived by the Holy Spirit, and that he is named Jesus because "he will save his people from their sins" (Matt 1:20, 21). We know, and he knows, that he, there along the Sea, is the beloved Son of the one whose voice came from heaven. You can say with all truth that Jesus is the original icon of the Trinity in whom all the fullness of God pleases to dwell bodily (see Col 1:19, 2:9).

There is no question of Jesus having a vocation. He was not called; rather, as the gospel passage we are about to consider shows, he is the caller (#5). Noah was called, Abraham was called, Moses was called, Samuel was called, David was called; Isaiah, Jeremiah, Amos were called, Paul was called, and now Peter and Andrew, and soon James and John, are called. Vocation is a recurring divine method in the Bible. Even creation in Genesis 1 is an act of vocation, "Let there be."

As Matthew presents him, though, Jesus was not called. He did not receive a vocation. He wasn't even "called from the womb."

Jesus did not receive a mission; he was sent with one "to the scattered sheep of the House of Israel" (Matt 15:24), sent as the Sender (Matt 10:5-6). What he does is who he is; his mission, if you want to use that word, is himself in the world, Emmanuel, God-with-us. He does not worry about the morrow, he makes no plans, no provision for the future; rather, he illumines the *kairos* with his effective, evocative presence. In Matthew's account Jesus is not called, but proclaimed; not so much sent as manifested, indicated, and followed.

Going from Nazareth to Capernaum, Jesus descended from Galilee's higher elevations to the lake district below. Descending, looking down, he would have seen that the Sea of Galilee in the distance was shaped like a harp. From then on, the Sea and the life around it became for him a living psalter, in the way that Roman Catholic school children used to make living rosaries. Unlike a living rosary, though, the living psalter around the Sea of Galilee was real and not make-believe.

The Psalms and their melodies were as close to him as his heartbeat. With family and friends, from infancy on, there was always music to the Most High, proclaiming God's loving mercy in the morning, his truth in the night, on the ten-stringed lute, with the sound of song on the harp (see Ps 92:1-4).

Like a child in California, growing up ever seeing only a picture of a cardinal but never a live one, or a child in Ames ever seeing only a picture of the Pacific Ocean, so coming from inland Nazareth to the fertile lake district did Jesus come to Capernaum. Psalms that before had been just the stuff of imagination now came to life before Jesus' eyes: how it was true that the God in Sion fills the land with joy, visits the earth, softens it with showers, fills it with riches, blesses its growth, crowns the year with his bounty.

It was true, he saw, that the hills were girded with joy, the meadows clothed with flocks, the valleys decked with wheat, and he, too, shouted with joy, yes, he sang,

Cry out with joy to God, all the earth,
O sing to the glory of his name.
Let the sea and all within it thunder praise.
Let the land and all it bears rejoice. (see Pss 65, 66, 96)

One morning he got up as usual before the sun came over the eastern hills. The words rose with him from his bed: "My heart is ready, O God; my heart is ready. I will sing, I will sing your praise. Awake, my soul! Awake, lyre and harp! I will awake the dawn" (Ps 67:8-9).

After coffee, they went out.

I imagine: the morning air was warm, and Jesus saw the sun peak and rise. He noted, "it gives its light to the Gentile Gadarenes on the eastern bank, just as it does to us in the valley; in fact, its rays hit *their* land first and only *after* that the land of the Jews." The light glanced off the gold ring on his baby toe.

> Come, children, and hear me, that I may teach you the fear of the Lord?
> *Too presumptuous, maybe, even arrogant.*
> I will open my mouth in a parable and utter hidden lessons from the past?
> *That, too—for now, anyway, though the parable part has possibilities.*
> Glorify the Lord with me; together let us praise his name?
> *Yes.*

"He saw two brothers, Simon who is called Peter and Andrew his brother . . . and he said, 'Follow me'" (Matt 4:18, 19).

> What? No! Wait! Hey, it's working. They're coming. OK, then, this is it.

5

On Matthew 4:18-22

(Mark 1:16-20; see Luke 5:1-11;
see John 1:35-42)

Walking by the Sea of Galilee Jesus sees two men, Peter and his brother Andrew.

> They are casting a net into the sea.
> *They are fishermen.*
> I know that.

"Come after me," he says, directing himself to the two brothers, "and I will make you fishers of humans" (Matt 4:18, 19).

We can imagine the scene. Peter and Andrew are standing in the shallows just offshore casting the wide circular net that as it sinks to the bottom, maybe ten feet, will take with it whatever small fish will have come under it as it descends. One or both of the brothers will then dive down there and gather the perimeter of the net together, closing the fish in, and together they will haul the whole thing ashore.

There are many other fishermen along the lake doing the same, and two other brothers in the anchored boat just up shore. Peter and Andrew have other nets, some already full of silver shimmering fish, some that they will soon cast out like the one they just did. The brothers have stripped for the work so they are naked.

They do it all themselves.
They're barely making it.
It's thankless work.
Ha! You're only just beginning. A day at a time. Better, an hour.

Jesus has walked out toward the two brothers and is standing in the water within hearing distance. "Come after me," he says, "and I will make you fishers of humans."

Nothing.
Louder.

And he says it again. The two brothers grab their clothes and go in the direction of the words.

What? No! Wait!
See, it worked.
OK, then.

Something similar happens up shore with the two brothers in the boat, James and John. Their father is with them in the boat. Jesus calls them, but not their father, and the two sets of brothers begin to follow Jesus.

Jesus had said, "Come after me." *Come* is a verb of movement, and *after* is an adverb of place. In response, the brothers *begin to follow* him.[1] To *begin to follow* is neither merely movement nor merely spatial. It is relational not only in terms of position in space, but also in terms of interior and personal disposition and intentionality.

By beginning to follow Jesus, the brothers make Jesus their leader. We can speak of discipleship, though the New Testament does not use that word: the brothers make themselves learners in relationship to Jesus, who would be the Teacher, the rabbi, the master (see #39).

---

1. The aorist tense of the verb has the sense of starting to do something.

Furthermore, *beginning* implies continuing; beginning implies duration and the long haul. It is a Genesis word, and the brothers will remember that Jesus had said of them "I will make you."

Jesus' call, "Come after me," was like the word at the beginning when God created: "Let there be." And the brothers' response of *beginning to follow* was their re-creation, their starting life anew along the freshwater lake that is called a sea, recalling the primal chaos that was the setting of the first creation (Gen 1:1-3).

Each set of brothers left something, Peter and Andrew their nets, and James and John the boat and their father. Discipleship of Jesus arose through a call that is often described as peremptory. *Peremptory* comes from the Latin *perimere,* which means to kill or destroy. Jesus' call puts an immediate end to the past.

The net that Peter and Andrew had just cast would be lying ten feet below the surface, holding captive a plethora of terrorized fish that would die there slowly and uselessly. They would have died all the same had they been pulled ashore, but not uselessly. Now, the brothers' day's work was made a waste, their past and future hopes irrelevant to the new present that had come upon them.

What was *that* about, the brothers wondered? The thought of those trapped fish put their hair on end when they remembered Jesus' words to them: "I will make you fishers of humans." Who was this guy with this grotesque, not-very-funny plan—for *us*? How will he "make" us? Do we want to be *made*? Is this some kind of new creation, a start-up scheme?

These two net-casting fishermen suddenly felt themselves caught, fished, but by what cords? There's a hymn that goes,

> *They cast their nets in Galilee*
> *Just off the hills of brown*
> *Such happy simple fisherfolk*
> *Before the Lord came down.*

It goes on to say that God's peace filled their hearts but *broke them too*, that John died alone in Patmos and Peter was crucified upside down. The hymn ends,

> *The peace of God, it is no peace,*
> *But strife closed in the sod.*[2]

"Jesus saw two brothers" (Matt 4:18; see #21). Matthew identifies them as fishermen (Matt 4:18), but Jesus saw "brothers," family and community, not function and career. That they were brothers must have given them added value in Jesus' eyes. Was his choice of two sets of brothers as his first disciples a symbolic gesture toward the healing of an old pattern of sibling rivalry in his own people—Abel and Cain, Isaac and Ishmael, Jacob and Esau—a pattern that Jesus always thought was a waste of energy? Was he saying, "Let's get beyond that, in the kingdom of God!"

Two sets of two brothers makes four disciples. Four was for all directions, like the psalm that compared Torah to the sun, its voice going forth through all the earth, its message to the utmost bounds of the world (Ps 19). "At least in my lifetime," Jesus might have thought, "it could reach the Gadarenes and Tyre and Sidon" (see Matt 8:28; 15:21).

"Come after me and I will make you fishers of humans." In the gospel of Matthew this is the third word of Jesus, apart from his dialogue with Satan during the forty days in the desert. The first word was to the Baptist—"Let it be so now, for thus it is fitting for us to fulfill all righteousness" (Matt 3:15)—and the second was "Repent, for the kingdom of heaven is at hand" (Matt 4:17). Now he says, "Come after me and I will make you fishers of humans."

Each of the three words has two parts. It looks as though the first part is a command and the second part the explanation for it, or its consequence: Let it be . . . because; Repent . . . because;

2. William Alexander Percy (1885–1942), "They cast their nets in Galilee," *Lutheran Book of Worship* (Minneapolis, MN: Augsburg, 1978), #449.

Come after me . . . and. Does Jesus always speak this way? You can check it out as you do your *lectio* of the gospels and listen to the Gospel proclaimed at Mass.[3]

A way to understand this manner of speaking is to remember that Jesus was a Jew, and his education was based on Bible stories, and especially on the Psalms.

The Psalms and the prophets are always saying things in pairs; if something is worth saying once, then it's worth saying twice. Open the Psalter and all kinds of examples of this come to meet you: "They surround me all the day like a flood; together they close in against me," "O Lord, you have lifted up my soul from the grave, restored me to life from those who sink into the pit" (Pss 88:17; 30:4), and, as we just saw, "their sound through all the earth, their message to the bounds of the world" (Ps 19:4).

Bible scholars call this way of talking parallelism. It means that the second part is more or less a repetition in different words of the first part. So when Jesus says to these brothers, "Come after me and I will make you fishers of humans," they understood that this was not two things but one, that the second part was what the first part would look like in their lives from now on: for them to come after Jesus was to be fishers of humans.

In contemporary terms we can say that to be a disciple is to be given a mission, and vice versa. In addition we can say that Jesus' call of the four brothers was directly related to his immediately preceding word: "Repent, for the kingdom of heaven is at hand." And so at one point when someone says, "I will follow you wherever

---

3. *Lectio*—*Lectio divina* means "the holy reading of holy things." It is reading (or listening to) the Bible (the holy thing) with the desire to hear what God is saying to you and to your community through his Word. You want to devote time to *lectio*, say twenty minutes a day, and you want to do it in an atmosphere of silence, preferably in the company of others. In twenty minutes you might actually "read" no more than a phrase or two. When you are struck (not stuck), then stop, wonder, listen, and give thanks. Finally, ask, "What have I heard, and what do I do about it?"

you go," Jesus tells him, "No one who puts his hand to the plow and looks back is fit for the kingdom of God" (Luke 9:61, 62).

Jesus' call is peremptory and embraces all the directions of our lives, putting them in the service of the kingdom of heaven, which Jesus would compare to a dragnet. The kingdom of God is a fishing business, now up and running and in competition with the king of Babylon, of whom the prophet Habakkuk had said that to him men were "like the fish in the sea . . . without a leader. He brings them all up with a hook, hauls them away with his net, and then rejoices and exults" (Hab 2:14-15).

> He has franchises everywhere; he controls the market. What can four guys and a Messiah do?
> *Ask your mother what good a little yeast does against all that coarse flour. Oh, I forgot; you left her, didn't you? Knowing you, that was peremptory.*

They went on, then, to whatever would come next.

6

On Matthew 4:23-25

(Luke 6:17–19; see Mark 1:35–39)

I am always in your presence. You are holding me by my
    right hand.
There's a cup in my hand, full of wine.
It is *you* who are my portion and cup.
You will drink it to the dregs.
All the wicked on the earth must drain it.
Even so.

Jesus called the four fishermen to come after him, and they
began to follow him (#5). But then there is no mention of these
four when with three verses Matthew next shows Jesus going
about all of Galilee, teaching in their synagogues and preaching
the Gospel of the kingdom and healing every disease and infirmity
among the people (Matt 4:23-25).

In these three verses in chapter four Matthew shows who Jesus
is by showing what he does: he is loving Jesus. As the gospel of
Matthew unfolds we will understand that these three verses are
an *exemplum*. Saint Paul would say, "Be imitators of me as I am
of Christ" (1 Cor 11:1; see 1 Cor 4:16). The gospel is mimetic,
that is, it works and spreads by imitation. "I have given you an
example," Jesus said after administering to those whom he loved
to the end the sacrament of the washing of the feet, "that you also

should do as I have done to you"; "even as I have loved you, so you also, love one another" (see John 13:1-15).

Saint Benedict knew this principle of imitation. The abbot "must point out . . . all that is good and holy more by example than by words" (RB 2.12). We know that it is not only the abbot who teaches by example. All members of the community are evangelizers to one another, witnesses to God's grace "by living example" (RB 2.12), at the bare minimum doing what should be done and not doing what should not be done. The eighth degree of humility in Saint Benedict's Rule is that "a monk does only what is endorsed by . . . the example set by his seniors" (RB 7.55).

We have to remember that Jesus did not preach Christianity. He did not found a religion. He proclaimed the kingdom of God. Jesus' preaching was *performative*, meaning that his very preaching of the kingdom of God made the Mystery present.

We notice the catholicity of Jesus' mission: "all" of Galilee, "all" of Syria, "all" the sick, and not just one synagogue but "their synagogues," each and every one.

We notice, too, along with this wide embrace, a simultaneous and parallel zeroing in. I refer in these three verses in Matthew to the use of the preposition *in*. Jesus goes around "in" all of Galilee, he teaches "in" their synagogues, and he heals every disease that is "in" all the people. Jesus covers ground from the geo-political— Galilee—through the socio-religious—synagogues—to the intimately personal—the ailments in all the people, in every person.

Saint Matthew is describing the place of the church in the world. The church too is catholic, and because it is catholic it also touches each soul intimately and personally, healing that soul as if it were the only soul in the universe by bringing that soul into sacramental and real communion with all other souls touched by the Word and by the Grace that she mediates.

And what about a monastic community? "To you, therefore, my word is directed," says Saint Benedict early in the Prologue, addressing a single soul, but only so that at the end of the Rule

Benedict can say with unqualified assurance, "may Christ lead us all together—*nos pariter*—to eternal life" (RB Pro 2; 62.12).

Jesus had told Simon and Andrew that he would make them fishers of humans. If they were looking on at a distance to see how it was done they would have seen that Jesus fished by attraction. They would have learned, as Pope Benedict often said, that that is the church's method: attract rather than coerce or trap or command. Jesus did not use lures or nets; he was the lure that was also the reward that the attraction promised. "Report of him spread everywhere" (Matt 4:24).

Matthew reports two things that Jesus did: he preached the Gospel, and he healed disease and infirmity. Later, Matthew will in some detail tell us the content of Jesus' teaching: the Sermon on the Mount, his instructions to the Twelve, the parables, his instructions for the church, and his warnings of final Judgment. But here, in these three verses, Matthew does not tell us the content of Jesus' teaching.

By contrast, in these same three verses Matthew says twice that Jesus healed and then underlines that fact with nine different words about Jesus' healing. There is such an emphasis on healing in these three introductory verses in Matthew that it would be easy to conclude that it was by healing rather than by words that Jesus declared that the kingdom of God had come. Healing performed the fact that the kingdom was near, that is, that it was not far.

This conclusion makes sense when we recall that in the ancient world sickness was a sign of the triumph of the Evil One and also of the nearness of death and of death's irrevocable claim on those it visits. But both of these realities, the Evil One and Death's finality, were hallmarks of that other kingdom, the one that the kingdom of God was opposed to.

Besides illness and disease in general and of every kind, Matthew names three maladies in particular. Demoniacs were under the influence of alien powers, those who will later ask Jesus, "Have you come here to torment us before the time?" (Matt 8:29). Lunatics, or the moonstruck, were under the power of nonhuman creation somehow become hostile to humankind. And the lame were victims simply of the failing human flesh that every child of Adam will finally see exhaust itself.

Finally, Jesus healed pains. Jesus noticed and apparently distinguished among pains. For him, pain was particular and personal, specific and nontransferable. Your pain is you, not me, and Jesus addressed pains.

Jesus was not at all resigned before pain as a way for people to transcend themselves. For Jesus, pains and illnesses were brand marks that the enemy—death and the devil—imposed on his captive spoils. The kingdom Jesus proclaimed was a reversal of the hostage situation.

In any case, I think we understand that Jesus' healing of illnesses and pains is similar to his raising the dead to life. The son of the widow of Nain will die again (Luke 7:11-15), and so will Lazarus (John 11:38-44) and the twelve-year-old girl Jesus raised back to life (Mark 5:39-42). So pains will return, and illnesses too, and lunatics will again be susceptible to the pull of the moon.

Just as eternal life is not the same as biological life prolonged without end, neither is kingdom-health and well-being the same as what you can have with Advil Extreme.

Jesus' exorcisms and his healing of pains and illnesses point beyond themselves to the dawning of the kingdom of heaven. They are, like his preaching, signs that the kingdom is not far but near, God's imminent triumph over evil, or, as Jesus will say later on, his healings are acts of violence, plundering the strong man's house after binding him, because "the kingdom of God has come upon you" (Matt 12:28-29).

Ben Meyer makes the point that Jesus' healings addressed to specific people's personal illnesses and pains "signified the reign of God in a way that illuminated its relation to world and history and bodily life precisely as fulfillment; . . . not the mere end but the consummation and re-creation of the world."[1] Saint Paul

---

1. Ben F. Meyer, *The Aims of Jesus* (London: SCM, 1979), 154–58.

would put it this way—same melody, different key: "Where sin increased, there grace super-abounded" (Rom 5:20).

The four disciples would have noticed that there was no selection process, no triage. It was the sickness alone that merited the healing. I wonder, can I do that, not with a crowd, but with just the fifteen brothers I live with?

Saint Benedict suggests a modest imitation of Jesus: "support with the greatest patience one another's weaknesses of body or behavior." He adds that doing that is a form of obedience, and I would say obedience to the opportunity that the sick brother is (RB 72.5, 6).

> What man can live and never see death?
> *The Lord will help you on your bed of pain, will bring you back from sickness to health.*
> My life is spent with sorrow . . . my bones waste away.
> *Be still, and know that I am God*

7

On Matthew 5:1-3

I remarked above that in Matthew 4:23-25 there is such an emphasis on healing that it would be easy to conclude that for Matthew, and even more for Jesus, it was healing rather than words that declared that the kingdom of God had come (#6).

I think this observation that it was mainly through wordless action rather than through speech that Jesus proclaimed the kingdom of God is implied in the very next scene in Matthew. It is the beginning of the Sermon on the Mount. Matthew says not only that Jesus taught but that "he opened his mouth and taught them" (Matt 5:2). The Sermon on the Mount is oral, verbal teaching about the kingdom, parallel to and maybe even secondary to the nonverbal acting out of the nearness of the kingdom of God in Jesus' ministry.

"Seeing the crowds, he went up the mountain." Jesus' going up the mountain is a response to his seeing the crowds. Jesus did not wake up that morning with a plan: "Today I am going up that mountain and giving a three-chapter-long sermon." No doubt he had an idea, but he didn't have a plan. He was poor in spirit and clean of heart; he had no agenda in the way that we speak of agendas, something we intend to push on others by force or manipulation or charm.

The kingdom of God was not an agenda; it was the announcement of a promise fulfilled, the reality and true interpretation of everything, the answer to mourning and hunger and thirst and the reason for mercy and for making peace.

Jesus saw the crowds, and so he went up the mountain. His disciples came to him, and opening his mouth he taught them. (We note in passing that the same three things, the mountain, the disciples, and teaching, occur again at the very end of the gospel of Matthew. There, on the mountain, Jesus tells the disciples, "Go, therefore, . . . teaching" [Matt 28:16, 19].) Here, the idea that he had, the kingdom of God, began to take shape as he taught on the mountain, and his act of teaching was compelled by his seeing the crowd.

It's like when John in his gospel tells of the time Philip and Andrew told Jesus that some Greeks had said to Philip, "Sir, we would like to see Jesus" (John 12:20-23). When Jesus heard that, he knew that "the hour has come for the Son of Man to be glorified," and very shortly afterward he was crucified so that he might draw all to himself.

You never know when you will see something or hear something that will catapult you in the blink of an eye from having an idea or a hope to the realization of that hope and the enfleshment of that idea in some bold and even frightening way of acting. You can say that this being catapulted is a second conversion that intrudes upon you unbidden just when you were either settled into a complacent routine or getting bored by it.

The New American Bible Revised Edition cheats us, because it leaves out "He opened his mouth." Instead, it paraphrases with "He began to teach." It is like leaving out "with the kisses of his mouth" from the opening of the Song of Songs, "as if," Saint Bernard explains such a supposed omission, "lovers should kiss by means other than the mouth" (SC 1.5; CF 4:3).[1] How else can someone teach except by opening his mouth?

---

1. Saint Bernard of Clairvaux (1090–1153). Through his own monastery talks and his treatises Saint Bernard developed and transmitted the humanistic, Christ-centered, mysticism of love that has characterized Cistercian spirituality

Well, as we saw a moment ago, first of all by his deeds. Saint Benedict says that the abbot should teach more by example than by words. So Matthew says, "he opened his mouth," to emphasize that the teaching to follow is oral, like this talk. The 1964 film *The Gospel According to Matthew* by Pier Paolo Pasolini makes the point when the camera frames only Jesus' face as he delivers the entire Sermon on the Mount.

But maybe also Saint Matthew means to call to our mind the very Song of Songs, "His speech is most sweet" (Song 5:16), and also the Royal Wedding Song, Psalm 45:3: "you are the fairest of the sons of men, and graciousness is poured upon your lips, because God has blessed you forevermore." Saint Luke says that the people of Nazareth "were amazed at the gracious words that came from his mouth" (Luke 4:22). That was before they tried to throw him off the cliff.

As Jesus used his hands to touch people's ears and tongue and eyes, and to take them by the hand and raise them up, and to break bread and pass it to others, so he used his mouth to speak. His mouth, a part of his body, touched the words he spoke before those words reached others' ears. The words, chewed by his mouth, were warmed by his lips and had the flavor of his breath when they reached and entered the crowds who watched and listened. "His lips drip flowing myrrh" (Song 5:13).

Opening his mouth he taught them, saying, "Happy the poor in spirit because the kingdom of heaven is theirs" (Matt 5:3). That is Jesus' idea taken shape, which his seeing the crowds elicited from him.

If it were just that one statement, it would have seemed a disappointing beginning. You might have thought that telling a parable, which Jesus would show himself good at, would have been a better opening than "Happy the poor in spirit because the kingdom of

---

to the present day. Noteworthy among his works are his eighty-six sermons on the Song of Songs (CF 4, CF 7, CF 31, CF 40), and his treatise on loving God (CF 13 and CF 13B).

heaven is theirs." Or why didn't he at least put it in direct address, in second person, saying as he looked into their eyes, "Happy are *you* who are poor in spirit, for the kingdom of heaven belongs to *you* . . . and to you . . . and to you"?

Instead he puts it in the third person plural, "the poor" and "their." It is an abstract, general statement that sounds more like a theorem than a proclamation.

On the other hand, if Jesus had said, "Happy are you," it could have come across as condescending. By putting it in the third person Jesus was, in fact, turning a divine principle into a proclamation, a proclamation that the crowds could not only embrace as directed *to them*, but also in their turn could proclaim to *others*, down through the ages to our own day. As Pope Francis so often reminds us, the church is not only a church for the poor: it is a church of the poor. And, again, these are words from Jesus' mouth, so they contain and bring with them something of him if not all of him.

Also, this is not just one statement. These first words from Jesus' mouth constitute the first brief member of a litany of eight similarly brief members that in their staccato rhythm have an accumulating effect. We call these the eight Beatitudes. You can imagine Jesus singing this litany in rap style and after the second or third verse the crowd joining in to sing along with him, "Happy are," "Happy are," repeated like a refrain.

The Beatitudes then certainly had their effect, uniting the crowd in joy and song and making them feel what the words themselves proclaimed, that they were most fortunate, happy, and that God was for them all the way.

At the end of the Sermon on the Mount, in any case, the crowds are "astonished" at his teaching (Matt 7:38), in its effect authoritatively bringing them to a new experience of themselves and of one another and opening up possibilities hidden in their poverty and sorrow that had seemed before then impossible precisely because of their poor condition.

Jesus in his Beatitudes, and in his entire proclamation in deed and word, was saying, as Pope Francis has said, that God "needs our eyes to see the needs of our brothers and sisters. He needs our hands to offer them help. He needs our voice to protest the injustices committed."[2]

Poor in spirit means poor with respect to the Holy Spirit. It is behind Paul's saying, "the Spirit comes to the aid of our weakness" (Rom 8:26). Jesus is the one Isaiah had in mind when he said, "The spirit of the Lord God is upon me . . . to bring good news to the afflicted," healing to broken hearts, liberty to captives, comfort to those who mourn (Isa 61:1-2).

To be poor in spirit means to be in that condition alone on which the spirit of the Lord God can shower its godly gifts. I think J. B. Phillips got it right when he translated this verse, "Happy are those who know their need for God."[3] Paul put it this way: "I will gladly boast of my weaknesses, that the power of Christ may rest upon me" (2 Cor 12:9).

Speaking of the Beatitudes globally, Pope Francis says, "We can only practice them if the Holy Spirit fills us with its power and frees us from our weakness, our selfishness, our complacency, and our pride."[4] To be poor in spirit is, negatively, to be empty of self so as, positively, to be filled up with the gifts of God, the Wisdom of God, the power of God, the foolishness of God.

You can develop poverty of spirit in very simple ways by checking your tendency to manipulate things to your own comfort. Manipulation of things to suit ourselves is a nonverbal form of murmuring. There is something innocent about receiving what is given without modifying the gift to suit us, or doing what is asked without putting conditions on the request. Benedict talks about being content with the poorest and the worst, which simply means

---

2. Reported by Hannah Brockhaus, CNA Catholic News Agency, September 7, 2018; https://www.catholicnewsagency.com/news/39314/speak-out-against -injustice-pope-francis-says.

3. J. B. Phillips, *The New Testament in Modern English* (New York: Macmillan, 1958).

4. GE 65.

being content with the way things are, the point being the contentment (RB 7.49).

Practicing contentment in this way, we begin to prepare ourselves to be poor in spirit. In fact, I don't know how anyone can ever become a contemplative without being poor in spirit in this way, attentive for God even before an open window that you could easily reach out and close against the draft; close the window: you've precluded the gift. For those who love God, everything cooperates for the good (Rom 8:28).

8

On Matthew 5:3-11

(Luke 6:20-22)

Jesus opens the Sermon on the Mount with the Beatitudes. You can find all kinds of commentaries on the Beatitudes. The best commentary on the Beatitudes is Jesus himself. I don't mean his oral teaching so much as his interior dispositions and attitudes.

You can see his interior dispositions and attitudes in his non-verbal responses to people and situations. Sometimes you have to read between the lines with some imagination to notice these interior dispositions of Jesus. But they are not foreign to us, and if we are honest we can find many of these interior dispositions and attitudes within ourselves, if only in the form of our *desire* for them, when instead we respond to people and situations with their painful opposites and compunction creates the desire for something better.

Sometimes the evangelist helps: "He was moved with pity," "He looked at him and loved him," "He looked around with anger," "He was silent." The third chapter of Pope Francis's recent Apostolic Exhortation, *Gaudete et Exultate: On the Call to Holiness in Today's World*, shows how the Beatitudes provide a portrait of Jesus that we are called to reflect in our daily lives. Each of the Beatitudes is an example of holiness. "The Beatitudes are like a Christian's identity card," he says.[1]

---

1. GE 63.

Francis seems to be repeating what the Catechism says. The title of part three of the Catechism is "Life in Christ." Article two, "Our Vocation to Beatitude," says that the Beatitudes "are at the heart of Jesus' preaching," "depict the face of Jesus Christ," "portray his charity," and "shed light on the actions and attitudes characteristic of Christian life."[2]

I was reflecting on the Beatitudes in Matthew at the same time that I was reading over chapter seven of the Rule of Saint Benedict, the twelve steps of humility. You might call the twelve steps in RB 7 the monk's identity card.

Here we have two lists, one the sources and expressions of happiness or blessedness, the other the sources and expressions of humility, but I don't think you can make any convincing distinction between evangelical blessedness and Benedictine humility. The happy (blessed) person is humble, and the humble person is happy. There's no need to complicate things beyond conforming yourself to the grace that comes to you along so many ways by the Holy Spirit.

Maybe all the Beatitudes after the first one are simply that one in other words: poor in Spirit, understood as poor with respect to the Holy Spirit, meaning knowing your need for God.

The Beatitudes embrace two time zones, now and the future, *being* in a certain way *now* in view of something in the *future*: Blessed are those who mourn [now], for they *shall be* comforted, literally, Paracleted.

It's a deferred reward, it seems, except that the present/future pattern does not hold for the first and last Beatitudes. There, the promise is *already* fulfilled: Blessed are the poor in spirit [now], blessed are those who are persecuted for righteousness' sake [now], for theirs *is* the kingdom of heaven [now] (Matt 5:3, 11). We can go a long way on that conviction, and suffer a lot, so that deferred

2. CCC 1716, 1717.

rewards are the material of the theological virtue of hope, which does not disappoint.

Paul puts this conviction this way: first listing all kinds of possibilities for despair, he concludes, "I am sure that" none of these or things like them "will be able to separate us from the love of God in Christ Jesus our Lord," which love is the same as the kingdom of God (Rom 8:38, 39).

See again the seventh chapter of the Rule of Saint Benedict. If you asked me to summarize the Beatitudes in one of the degrees of humility it would be the sixth: that a monk is content with things from WalMart and things past their use-before date, and in whatever is put on his shoulders he considers himself as if he were a disaster as a day laborer and undeserving, saying to himself, "I am reduced to nothing, a mule tethered at your door, and I am with you always" (RB 7.49-50).

9

On Matthew 5:11-12

(Luke 6:22-23; see John 15:18–16:4)

We have been reflecting on what are traditionally called the Beatitudes, which open the Sermon on the Mount in the gospel according to Saint Matthew.

That word we use, *Beatitudes*, is a noun. It refers to the genre or the form of speech. It is common in the Bible. The Psalter begins with a beatitude: "Blessed indeed is the man" (Ps 1:1). Jesus used this way of talking a lot: "Blessed is he who takes no offense in me"; "Blessed are you, Simon Bar Jona"; "Blessed are those who have not seen and yet believe" (Matt 11:6; 16:17; John 20:29).

But Jesus did not use the word *beatitude*. He never said, "Listen to another beatitude," in the way that he said, "Hear another parable" (Matt 21:33). Rather, we and church tradition came up with the title *the Beatitudes* for this litany of nine exclamations, each of which begins with the word *blessed*, or *happy*.

The word *blessed* (*makarios* in Matthew's Greek) is an adjective. It is predicated of someone as a quality of that person. In the Sermon on the Mount, it is a quality that comes as a gift from God. Then the quality becomes identified with someone, say, the poor in spirit or the pure of heart; in that way, the person himself becomes beatitude, happiness, blessedness.

Gregory of Nyssa asks what exactly beatitude is, and says that it "is a possession of all things held to be good, from which nothing is absent that a good desire may want." So "the one thing truly blessed is the Divinity Itself. . . . It is beatitude . . . inexpressible beauty . . . grace itself . . . , the fount of all goodness . . . the one thing lovable . . . rejoicing without end in infinite happiness."[1]

But because we are made in God's image, we enjoy beatitude too, inasmuch as we participate in God's beatitude: "human nature, which is the image of the transcendent beatitude, is itself marked by the beauty of goodness."[2]

I don't think Jesus had all this in mind when he called someone blessed, but he wouldn't deny what Gregory says, either. On the contrary, what Gregory said about beatitude applied to Jesus before it applied to anyone else. Not only was he in the image of God, he is the image of God, reflecting God's glory and bearing the very stamp of his nature (Heb 1:3).

I think that sometimes Jesus encountered someone whose evident beauty in humility caught him off guard, whose faith and courage totally endeared that person to Jesus. Then a beatitude spontaneously emerged from Jesus. It was both a public proclamation and a personal blessing.

That beatitudes were spontaneous and habitual with Jesus shows that he himself was a spontaneously happy soul, in no way morbidly self-conscious and guarded, but rather free, and taking delight in the children of Adam.

The ninth Beatitude is different from the others (Matt 5:11-12). It is about three times as long as the others, and it is addressed specifically to "you," whereas the other eight are not addressed to anyone but are declarations about persons with certain spiritual qualities. The ninth Beatitude is addressed to "you" plural, all of you, probably in the first instance Jesus' disciples who came to him when he sat down (Matt 5:1), and then to every Christian liturgical assembly ever after where this gospel is proclaimed.

---

1. Gregory of Nyssa, *On the Beatitudes* 1; trans. and annotated by Hilda C. Graef, Ancient Christian Writers 18 (New York: Newman, 1954), 87.

2. Gregory of Nyssa, *On the Beatitudes* 1; Graef, ACW, 87.

So this Beatitude is addressed to us: "Blessed are you."

Another difference with the ninth Beatitude is the addition of "when," implying a condition. The poor in spirit and the merciful, for instance, are always blessed just because of who they are, but in this case it is somehow contingent on something happening to us: "Blessed are you *when* they revile you and persecute you and say every bad thing against you falsely because of me" (Matt 5:11). When is that, and who are they who do these things, and why are those things the conditions of blessedness (see #10)?

10

On Matthew 5:11

(Luke 6:22; see John 15:18–16:4)

"Blessed are you *when* they revile you and persecute you and say every bad thing against you falsely because of me" (Matt 5:11).

This is the ninth Beatitude of the litany of Beatitudes that Jesus starts the Sermon on the Mount with in Matthew's gospel. We saw that, differently from the preceding eight, this one is addressed to "all of *you*" (#9).

We can imagine Jesus suddenly turning his eyes on those sitting closest to him and looking at them both globally and individually, sort of like what a priest tries to do at Mass when he says, "The Lord be with you," not with each one of you, but the Lord be with all of you together, then also with each one of you, too, but only as belonging to the all. Jesus is addressing his disciples, in whose midst he is when they are gathered together in prayer and works of mercy.

"When they revile you," etc. Jesus does not say *if*, but "when." The reviling of his disciples is certain; also the persecuting and the lies about bad things.

The only reason Jesus gives for this certainty is "because of me." What this "because" means is that Jesus' disciples are his surrogates, his emissaries, his representatives, his substitutes—his apostles, sent by him to be him, sheep among wolves (see Matt 10:16, 40). If we respond to Jesus' call "Follow me," then we will be him, and what they did to him they will do to us: a disciple is no greater than his master (John 13:16).

We are scapegoats of Jesus, and we thought that Jesus was our scapegoat. We suffer because of what he started, filling up in our own bodies what is lacking to the suffering of his—for the sake of his body (see Col 1:24).

In the eighth Beatitude Jesus had just said, "Blessed are those who are persecuted because of righteousness." Persecution is in both the eighth and the ninth Beatitudes, and so is "because of." The law of parallelism, then, means that "me," that is, Jesus, in the ninth, and "righteousness" in the eighth are synonymous. Jesus himself is the righteousness for whose sake his disciples will be reviled and persecuted, and have bad things said about them falsely. Saint Paul said, "He is . . . our wisdom, our righteousness and sanctification and redemption" (1 Cor 1:30).

"When they revile you," etc. Jesus does not say who "they" are, only that "they" did the same thing "to the prophets before you." If a prophet is one who speaks for God, then maybe the persecutors are those who do not hear, or, closer to the truth, those who do not like what they hear.

This idea of being reviled and persecuted for Jesus, for righteousness, for the kingdom of God, for the Gospel, does not make any of that—the Gospel, the kingdom of God, righteousness, Jesus—at all attractive. Here's how Pope Francis puts it in his Apostolic Exhortation *Gaudete et Exultate*: Jesus warns us that people who take the path he proposes will be nuisances in society. Yet "unless we wish to sink into an obscure mediocrity, let us not long for an easy life, for 'whoever would save his life will lose it' (*Mt* 16:25)."[1] Francis adds that "the Beatitudes are not easy to live out; any attempt to do so will be viewed negatively, regarded with suspicion, and met with ridicule."[2]

1. GE 90.
2. GE 91.

All the more can you expect this kind of negative response to Gospel beatitude and joy in a time when the love of many has grown cold (see Matt 24:12). Christians live under a death sentence.

I like equating Jesus with righteousness. Otherwise, I don't respond to the word *righteousness*. But when you think of Jesus as righteousness, or even of his foster father, Joseph, who was a righteous man (Matt 1:19), then you know you are just talking about a way of relating to people and a way of relating to God, which is what we mean by religion and which Jesus summed up as "love God with your whole heart and soul, and love your neighbor as yourself" (see Matt 22:37, 39).

Righteousness is simply being honest and bearing yourself with your God-given dignity as a child of God. Then you know that you're talking about the love that does not seek its own interest but that of others in eucharistic service.

Monks try to live righteously, so we can expect reviling, persecution, and bad things said against us falsely. Our thoughts and our memories revile and persecute us: you made a mistake, you could have had a family, you are wasting your time, you are becoming stale in lovelessness; God does not exist, the routine is killing me, the diet, too, and the loneliness of it. A member of our Order told me that when she was in an airport someone, noticing her monastic garb, said to her without malice but just as a fact, "You are a dying breed." Our persecuting thoughts and memories can be unrelenting, like the nails in the hands of a crucified man; they make for the slow martyrdom of the monk that Saint Bernard talks about, the yoke on the neck that is never lifted (see SC 30.11).

Note that Jesus does not say just "bad things" but "bad things falsely." Otherwise, he would be giving us permission to ward off any kind of criticism, any kind of calling us to account.

Sometimes we do "bad things" that need to be called out. Jesus says something about that in Matthew 18:15-17, a teaching Saint Benedict picked up (RB 23). For a brother to call them out might hurt us, but if he does it honestly as an act of speaking the truth in love, then he is not saying bad things falsely about us but calling us to a righteousness that exceeds that of the Pharisees—and precisely "on my account," that is, because of Jesus, who is our righteousness and the standard of our righteousness.

Within the memory of some, bad things were said against Cardinal Bernardin, falsely; then very recently the same kinds of bad things were said against Mr. (formerly Cardinal) Theodore McCarrick, but not falsely, and Jesus would not have it any other way.

Saint Peter asks, "Who is there to harm you if you are zealous for what is right? But even if you do suffer for righteousness' sake, you will be blessed. . . . It is better to suffer for doing right, if that should be God's will, than for doing wrong. . . . If you are reviled for the name of Christ, you are blessed" (1 Pet 3:13, 14, 17; 4:14). For that reason, because of that blessedness, "Rejoice and be glad, for your reward is great in heaven."

This—*Rejoice and be Glad*—is the title Pope Francis gave to his recent Apostolic Exhortation "on the call to holiness in today's world." He says, "The Lord asks everything of us, and in return he offers us true life, the happiness for which we were created. He wants us to be saints and not to settle for a bland and mediocre existence."[3]

Jesus talks about a great reward in heaven. But "heaven" is just a roundabout way of saying "God," and as many spiritual writers have said, God is an infinite circle whose center is everywhere and whose circumference is nowhere.

The reward is in God and can be nothing other than God, in whom we live, and move, and have our being, now (Acts 17:28). As Jesus will have us say in the prayer he will teach us, "your will be done, on earth as in heaven" (Matt 6:10).

To conclude, if the kingdom of God is the reward of the saints—"For theirs is the kingdom of God"—we note, too, that one of the Beatitudes is "Blessed are the pure in heart, for they

---

3. GE 1.

shall see God." But purity of heart and the kingdom of God are, according to John Cassian, respectively the *skopos* (the present goal) and the *telos* (the final end) of monastic life, the former anticipating the latter.[4] So monastic life, as Cassian and Benedict see it, is rooted in the spirituality and hope of the Beatitudes.

Who are the pure of heart who see God? It is those who ask, "Lord, when did we see you?" and get the reply, "what you did to the least of my brothers you did to me" (Matt 25:37, 40). Jesus calls them the righteous. And what is the kingdom of God if not the very world they live in and burnish, whose left hand in giving alms does not know what their right hand is doing (Matt 6:3)? It is the monk of perfect prayer, who does not understand himself or what he is praying.[5]

Happily, a Benedictine monastery is nothing but a community of the least of his brothers, with Jesus himself the least of them all (Luke 7:28). If you asked Saint Benedict, "Tell us in in a single sentence what you're getting at with your Rule," he'd say, in my opinion, just that: "What you did to the least of my brothers, you did to me" (RB 36.3; Matt 25:40). It is seeing God face to face, and pure prayer, and the kingdom of God on earth, from Vigils to Compline. It is also asking for persecution. Those "who were crucified with him reviled him in the same way" (Matt 27:44).

4. John Cassian, *Conference* 1.2, in Edgar C. S. Gibson, trans., *The Works of John Cassian*, Nicene and Post-Nicene Fathers of the Christian Church, 2nd series, vol. XI (Grand Rapids, MI: Eerdmans, 1978), 295.

5. See Cassian, *Conference* 9.31, in Gibson, *The Works*, 398.

11

On Matthew 5:13

(Mark 9:50; Luke 34-35)

With all the cucumbers coming in from the garden it seemed the honorable thing to do was to make dill pickles. I made two batches in a large earthenware crock. With the cucumbers I put in cloves of fresh garlic, a little turmeric, peppercorns, dried chili peppers, and sprigs of fresh dill, and then some grape leaves. The grape leaves are supposed to give the pickles a little crunch, a countermeasure against the liquid that they are submerged in.

So after putting all this into the crock, then you make brine and pour it in. You make the brine by dissolving sea salt in water. Brine is simply salt water. It's the salt that acts as a preservative for the pickles so that you can keep them in the crock, covered with the salty brine, for a year or so if you don't eat them all before that.

After he sings the Beatitudes in the Sermon on the Mount in Matthew, Jesus says to his disciples gathered there, "You are the salt of the earth" (Matt 5:13a).

It is an odd thing to say. You don't usually associate salt with earth but with the sea. At the very most, as Hilary of Poitiers says, it seems that being salt of the earth is nothing special.

Origen with others has pointed out that "salt preserves meats from decaying into stench and worms and makes them edible for a longer period of time."[1]

1. Hilary, On Matt 4.10; Origen, Fragment 91; both in ACCS 92.

But does the earth need to be preserved as raw meat or cucumbers do? Salt assists our taste buds so the flavor of food is enhanced. But is the earth food, so that salt on the tongue brings out its flavor?

Maybe Jesus was referring to the part in Genesis when "The Lord God took the man and settled him in the Garden of Eden, to cultivate and care for it" (Gen 2:15). The Garden of Eden is the earth, and cultivation and care are human activities directed to preserving and enhancing the garden.

So maybe that's it. Jesus used this quirky metaphor, salt of the earth, to remind his listeners of their original vocation to, as Pope Francis said with the title of his Encyclical *Laudato si'*, "care for our common home," the earth, which without that injunction could suffer as it actually has under humans' abuse and exploitation instead of being preserved and enhanced by our cultivation and care.

Saint John Chrysostom seems to agree with this interpretation, and then broadens it: "Why must you be salt? Jesus says in effect, 'You are accountable not only for your own life but also for that of the entire world. . . . I am sending you to the entire earth, across the seas, to the whole world" lest "all human nature itself" lose its taste. "Without the apostles' understanding and instruction, every soul is dull and unwholesome and unpleasant to God."[2]

We know today that salt, the sodium ion, doesn't so much change a food's flavor as it changes the person eating. Most people don't like bitter things too much. I remember a warm summer evening in the Sonora Desert in southwest Arizona being a guest of some people I had only recently gotten to know; before dinner they poured a generous glass of Campari over ice for each of us. I had never had Campari. It was bright red, and with the ice it looked really inviting, but a first sip made me cringe. Campari is bitter to the extreme. My hosts smiled as I took another sip; I was too polite to say it tasted like poison.

2. John Chrysostom, Hom on Matt 15.6; ACCS 92.

If you eat while you drink Campari, all you can taste is the Campari because it is the nature of bitterness to suppress other flavors. Here's where salt might have come in handy, but I didn't know that then. Had I only remembered the story of Elisha healing the death-dealing water by throwing salt into it (2 Kgs 2:19-22)! If something bitter takes control and suppresses other flavors, salt works on your taste buds by suppressing the receptor of bitterness. So in cooking foods whose natural bitterness can overpower more pleasant flavors, if you add a little salt, the salt subdues the bitterness and enhances your perception of more desirable flavors.

Another quality of salt, chemically speaking, is that it doesn't bind with anything. It just does its job and passes on.

Did Jesus know the modern account of the chemical properties of salt? Even if he didn't, his statement about his followers being the salt of the earth is no less wonderful and true.

His hope was, I think, that his disciples should be pilgrims on the earth, passing through, not carrying a moneybag or having anywhere to lay their heads. His hope was that their presence, which was the presence of the Holy Spirit within them, might suppress or even eliminate the overpowering effects of bitterness in the world and in people's lives and relationship. His hope was that their witness, the joy and hope and kindness of their presence, might change people's perception of reality so the good and the pleasing would come to the fore.

So salt preserves and salt enhances the truth of the world, of God's creation, of human interaction and history.

In a couple of places in the Pentateuch something like this is said: "it is the covenant of salt to last forever before the Lord" (e.g., Num 18:19). Salt is a symbol of covenant, and covenant is a binding agreement. In the ancient world, and maybe still today in some places, eating salt together at a meal was a sign of friendship or, on the political plain, of alliance and treaty. Jesus certainly knew of this custom. To be the salt of the earth, then, is to be an agent of friendship and concord, an instrument of peace in the world and in history.

The phrase I just used, *instrument of peace*, is from the prayer attributed to Saint Francis. You can hardly find a better description of what it means to be the salt of the earth, where salt neutralizes bitterness and forms bonds of love:

> Lord, make me an instrument of your peace.
> Where there is hatred, let me sow love;
> where there is injury, pardon;
> where there is doubt, faith;
> where there is despair, hope;
> where there is darkness, light;
> where there is sadness, joy.

I think the list of Instruments of the Spirit's Craft in chapter four of the Rule of Saint Benedict is along the same lines, and also chapter thirteen of Saint Paul's First Letter to the Corinthians. There, if you replace love with salt, then salt is patient, salt is kind, it is not rude, salt does not brood over injuries, and it rejoices in the truth. Jesus wants his metaphor to be turned into action, and these holy men show us how it is done.

We can ask, how can New Melleray Abbey continue being salt to the culture we live in, to the land of the church and the earth of history, at this moment in the twenty-first century, as we are about to mark one hundred seventy years on this land?[3] Maybe salt cannot lose its flavor, but it can fail to come out of the shaker when the humidity of routine or thoughtless habit, of aloofness, and of the iron mind of exclusivity impedes its passing through the little holes.

Or we can understand New Melleray Abbey as the land that receives salt to refresh, preserve, and enhance us. Our four Contemplative Experience participants, here for only a few weeks, are salt to us.[4] They just pass through, but by their respect and reverence,

---

3. New Melleray was founded in July of 1849.

4. Contemplative Experience is a program at New Melleray offering men a two- or three-week experience of monastic life.

by their questions and desires, by their suggestions and gentle prodding they open us to the sweet and pleasant, mitigating acidity and bitterness, traces of the "bad zeal" that Saint Benedict knows can poison community life (see RB 72.1).

The same can be said for Brother V. and for Brother M. C., men who enhanced New Melleray and helped to preserve it, not as a fossil, but as a living entity to go on living, whose memory lingers like a lovely fragrance after a pleasant presence has passed by and gone.[5]

5. Brother V. and Brother M. C.: One was a monk from another community of the Order who lived five years at New Melleray; the other underwent an initial monastic formation for five years but then discerned that his vocation was not to consecrated monastic life there.

12

On Matthew 5:14

"You are the light of the world" (Matt 5:14a). Is this a simple statement of the obvious? Do you recognize yourself in it? Are you obviously light? Are we a community of light, since Jesus uses the plural *you*? Is Jesus just saying what everyone can plainly see?

Or is "You are the light of the world" the revelation of something that has always been true but never been acknowledged or recognized, like the 2012 discovery of the Higgs boson, which has existed for billions of years but only now been identified?

Or is it a word that in its very speaking creates what it says, like that very first speech act in the Bible, when God spoke for the first time and said, "Let there be light, and there was light" (Gen 1:3)—so that in the same way that Saint Benedict talks about the monk's prompt obedience, the word is no sooner spoken than what it says is a fact, the two things happening, as it were, at once (see RB 5.9)?

If that is the case, then we are light of the world *because* Jesus said, "You are the light of the world." That interpretation makes a lot of sense to me.

"You are the light of the world." This statement in the Sermon on the Mount is parallel to the statement we considered in the previous talk: "You are the salt of the earth" (Matt 5:13). There are differences, though. Salt is an organic chemical compound, commonly sodium chloride, and likewise earth is largely chemicals and minerals. Light, though, is an electromagnetic wave-particle; and *the world*, in Matthew's Greek *kosmos*, is primarily a philosophical construct; *world* is the sum total of everything, the universe that God created and saw was good, ordered, and adorned with beauty.

As a creation of God, the *kosmos*, the world, is not God but everything that is other than God and that God loves.

Especially, the *kosmos*, the world, is humankind, as in the most quoted verse of Scripture, John 3:16: "God loved the *kosmos* so much that he gave his only Son . . . so that the *kosmos* might be saved through him" (John 3:16, 17). Commenting on Job 5:10, where God "sends water upon all things [*irrigat aquis universa*]," Gregory the Great says that *universa* denotes the human creature, in whom is "the true likeness and large participation [*communio*] of the universe."[1] In the experience of consciousness, the human creature "presents himself as an epitome of the cosmos, as a microcosm."[2]

"You are the light of the world," then, establishes a relationship between Jesus' disciples—we can say the church—and the entire created order.

Even more: is Jesus, in an audacious way, starting a new creation with his own version of "Let there be light," where now the light of the new creation is the community of his disciples, whom he also calls salt and leaven (Matt 5:13; see13:33)?

Light is a transverse wave. Ripples on water and ocean waves are also transverse waves. As light moves away from its source, it also oscillates like a carpet or a rope if you shake them. I guess you could say that light moves in three directions at the same time: up, down, and forward.

Light also has speed: in a vacuum, the speed of light is nearly three hundred million meters per second, or seven hundred million miles per hour. In a medium, light moves more slowly, depending on the medium. The effect of a medium on the speed of light is what we call refraction; it is responsible for our being able to see things.

---

1. Gregory the Great, Mor in Job 6.XVI.20.
2. Eric Voegelin, *Anamnesis*, trans. and ed. Gerhart Niemeyer (Notre Dame: University of Notre Dame Press, 1978), 28.

Some scientists say that "in the beginning" when God said "Let there be light," that is, in the very brief period immediately after the Big Bang, the speed of light was thousands of times faster than it is now; that is, the speed of light was faster than that than which nothing can be faster, that is, faster than light itself. If the universe is thirteen and a half billion years old, give or take twenty million years, you cannot blame light for slowing down a bit.

Anyway, at present the speed of light is considered a constant, that is, the speed of light in a vacuum. Atmosphere and things like glass and ice and water can slow it down, but nothing can speed it up.

Benedictine obedience, as I have said before, is like the speed of light. The master's order and the disciple's response are simultaneous, with the speed of the fear of God (see RB 5.8-9).

Sometimes, it is true, there will be something in the atmosphere to slow things down, some resistance usually rooted in pride and in one's own insecurity; in spite of our sincerely vowing ourselves to obedience to a rule and an abbot (RB 1.2), when it comes down to actual situations we want to be in charge of our life, even though Saint Paul and Saint Benedict say that we aren't and can't be; we even want to be in charge of *other* people's lives. We dominate when we can, we intimidate, we scold. But Benedict is always optimistic. He never stops hoping that the disciples' good will, and good sense, in the realm of monastic obedience will finally prevail.

We can say that prayer is like the speed of light, too. Pure prayer, I suppose, would be the speed of light in a vacuum, but most of us pray with some obstructions. Usually, our prayer is refracted. Whatever might be the case with physical light, our prayer is slowed down by distractions, by memories, by fantasies, by the awakening during the moments of quiet prayer of desires and yearnings for something other than God and that we hardly knew we had until we started to pray. It is as if the light that we are got split up by a prism and the pure unity was dispersed in all the colors of the spectrum.

Saint Bernard, for instance, states his intention when he goes to pray: "My heart speaks to you, my face has sought you: your face, Lord, I seek." But then, "Disaster for me, because of the un*clean*ness of my heart. It is what prevents me from deserving to be admitted to that happy vision. What care, my brothers, what zeal we must exercise, so that the eye with which we must look upon God may be cleansed. I feel myself defiled by a threefold uncleanness: the desires of the flesh, the desire for worldly glory, and the consciousness of past faults. For there are in my soul some motions of each desire that I cannot destroy by reason or force" (OS 1.13; see CF 54:142).

Echoing Bernard, here's Saint Aelred in a conference of his own addressed to the monks of Rievaulx (can you imagine living at Rievaulx with upwards to three hundred monks? Aelred retained everyone, as you can see by reading between the lines here): "What can I say, dear brothers? [Are we lights in heaven?] Are we in the same place that formerly Antony, Macarius, Hilary, and many others were? Or rather, have we not *fallen* from heaven to earth, we who taste almost nothing but earth, love the earth, think of the earth, speak of the earth, we who are contentious, argumentative, murmuring, biting at and devouring one another, envying and disparaging one another?" And he asks, "What are market days without monks?" which for us would mean, "How would HyVee survive without our regular visits there?"

On the other hand, in the same conference Aelred said that his brothers were indeed light, and stars in heaven, or could aspire to be: people who renounce the world, live in heaven in their thoughts and desires, people elevated above the entire world by their lives, customs, love, and contemplation, chaste in body, pure in mind, subjecting themselves to their superiors in humility and obedience, slow to anger, ready to serve, reluctant to receive, and never seeking their own but *what belongs to Jesus Christ*. These people, Aelred said, and he means us at New Melleray, too, are truly *lights of the world* (Oner 10.13, 14; see CF 83:98).

To conclude, light has both intensity and brightness: intensity in itself, brightness as perceived by and benefiting others. A light under a bushel basket is as intense as a light on a stand, but not as bright, because there is no one to perceive the light, no one to benefit from the light.

If by "Let your light shine" Jesus means let your brightness match your intensity, then he has given us a formula for the revitalization of our monasteries. Intensity would be what Saint Benedict calls good zeal (see RB 72.1): it would be unfeigned love, it would be the *intentio cordis*, the orientation of the heart of a monk devoted to simple silent prayer. Intensity would be undistracted serious *lectio*, zeal for the Work of God, and preferring nothing whatever to Christ. How can we as a community let our undoubted intensity shine always more brightly for a church and a world groping in the dark (see Bernard, SC 57.8)?

13

On Matthew 5:17-18

(Luke 16:17)

About whom was New Testament scholar John Meier talking when he said that his "pronouncements on legal/moral questions" were "ad hoc and unexplained"?[1]

Certainly, he was not talking about Pope Benedict, who never spoke off the cuff and who did nothing in his speaking and writing if not to explain things with the utmost care and clarity.

So he must have been talking about Pope Francis, whose *ad hoc* remarks like "who am I to judge" have been invoked by everyone from far left to far right to bolster their own peculiar legal and moral agenda.

But no, it wasn't Francis, either, whose pronouncements on legal and moral questions Meier said were *ad hoc* and unexplained.

It was, rather, Jesus that Meier was talking about.

But I think Meier's use of the word *pronouncements* is misleading. Jesus was a charismatic teacher. He was a contemplative who constantly read the book of creation and commented on that fundamental text as it opened itself to him in every moment.

It was particularly in his encounter with people that Jesus read the sacred text of creation.

1. John P. Meier, *A Marginal Jew*, vol. 4, *Law and Love* (New Haven: Yale University Press, 2009), 652.

I don't think Jesus made pronouncements on legal and moral questions. He did not pronounce; he proclaimed. Matthew summarizes everything in one sentence: "And he went about all Galilee teaching in their synagogues and preaching the gospel of the kingdom and healing every disease and every infirmity among the people" (Matt 4:23).

Ben Meyer says, "The words and actions of Jesus—the whole of his career . . . —were consciously and all-pervasively relative to the reign of God and its proclamation. . . . In Jesus, proclaimer and teacher were one. Proclamation determined teaching at every point and accounted for all its traits."[2]

In the Sermon on the Mount in Matthew's gospel Jesus says, "Do not think that I have come to abolish the law or the prophets. I have come not to abolish but to fulfill" (Matt 5:17). This is a proclamation of who Jesus is, and of the eternal will of God. "I have come not to abolish but to fulfill." It is an announcement of the world-changing event of the birth of the one who the angel told Joseph was going to "save his people from their sins" (Matt 1:21).

Maybe when Jesus said, "I have come not to abolish but to fulfill," he was in part trying to correct a false impression. That is why he first said, "Do not think that." The gospels make it clear that people talked about Jesus. More than once you read things like "A report concerning him went out through all the surrounding country" (Luke 4:11). Jesus had no control over what people were saying about him or thinking about him, and probably some of the reports carried the news that Jesus was a lawbreaker who encouraged his followers to break the Torah, too.

So when he says, "Do not think," he really means it: he knows that this is what many people were thinking, and he wants to set the record straight.

The question about Jesus' real attitude to the Torah is similar to the question of why Jesus was put to death. Setting aside

2. Ben F. Meyer, *The Aims of Jesus* (London: SCM, 1979), 137.

theological reasons, historically there is good reason to conclude that on the part of Jesus' executioners Jesus was put to death for political reasons: Jesus was regarded as a political revolutionary.

But there is also every reason to believe that on Jesus' part there was no politically revolutionary intention at all, except that the kingdom of God that he preached was near has political and social implications.

So the gospels show us Jesus involved in some pretty heated controversies with the scribes and Pharisees over legal and moral matters, yet if you look carefully at what he actually teaches about the law, it is hard to find what the legal authorities were so upset about.

For instance, Jesus said, "If any one comes to me without hating his father and mother, wife and children, brothers and sisters, and even his own life, he cannot be my disciple" (Luke 14:26). But he was not making a pronouncement on the Law; he was not abolishing the fourth commandment about honoring father and mother, and he was not abolishing the fifth commandment about murder, including suicide. He was, positively, in an *ad hoc* situation, driving home to would-be disciples the radical nature of his call to follow him.

When he said, "The Sabbath was made for man, not man for the Sabbath" (Mark 2:27), his intention was not to abolish the third commandment, and when he said, "Tax collectors and prostitutes are entering the kingdom of God before you," he was not abolishing the sixth and seventh commandments.

But people heard Jesus saying things like this over and over again, and they observed him doing things like healing people on the Sabbath and sitting at table with sinners and tax collectors.

It is not hard to imagine, then, that the report that "went out through all the surrounding country" would have included the judgment that Jesus was out actively to overthrow and abolish the Law. In community we misjudge each other's intentions all the time, but that's a topic for another occasion.

And so Jesus says in the Sermon on the Mount, first challenging that false judgment, "Do not think that I have come to abolish the law or the prophets," and then stating what he was really about: "I have come not to abolish but to fulfill."

But maybe the effect is the same. Does the way Jesus fulfills the Law have the effect after all of actually abolishing the Law?

They ask him, "Is it lawful for a husband to divorce his wife?" Jesus replies, "What did Moses [the Law] command you?" They answer, "To write a bill of divorce and give it to her." "Because of the hardness of your hearts," Jesus concludes, "he wrote you this commandment. But from the beginning of creation 'God made them male and female.' Therefore, what God has joined no human must separate" (see Matt 19:3–9; Deut 24:1; Gen 2:24).

Jesus fulfills the Law by rooting the intention of the Law in the eternal will, that is, in the intention, of God. But now, in your midst, in your hearing, the intention of God is here: as Jesus will say, "on earth as in heaven." The inner dynamism of Torah is realized; the external forms are rendered relative and even irrelevant.

By fulfilling the Law, Jesus abolishes the Law.

With the coming of the kingdom of God, continuing to "accept things as they are" and to "do things as we have always done," continuing to accommodate hard hearts and weak wills, no longer corresponds with reality.[3] Saint Paul puts it simply and clearly: "Christ is the end of the Law," "love is the fulfillment of the Law," and, "I, through the Law, have died to the Law, that I might live to God" (Rom 10:4; 13:10; Gal 2:19).[4]

---

3. Meyer, *The Aims of Jesus*, 139, 140, 143.

4. Religion is about taking the utmost care to establish and maintain connection with what is most important to you. Saint Paul uses the word *Law*, or *Torah*, I think, to mean "the religion of Judaism." For Paul, the Law was religion. When he says that the one who loves has fulfilled the Law he means that the love of God revealed in Jesus Christ has offered an end to religion by creating definitive bonds between human beings and God, and among human beings. Consequently, for those who take the offer, Christianity is not a religion. It is the end of religion, in both senses of end, finish and fulfillment. Christianity is the never-old and always surprising experience that is accessible to every person everywhere and is expressed in words Saint Paul gave us: "I live, no longer I, but Christ lives in me;

Jesus immediately adds, "Amen, I say to you, until heaven and earth pass away, not the smallest letter or the smallest part of a letter will pass from the law, until all things have taken place" (Matt 5:18). But the world has already passed away: "The meek . . . will inherit the land," and "You are the light of the world."

It is at his crucifixion that heaven and earth are revealed as having passed away: "From noon onward, darkness came over the whole land. . . . The veil of the sanctuary"—the symbol of the cosmos—"was torn in two . . . tombs were opened, and the bodies of many . . . were raised" (Matt 27:45, 51, 52-53), and so Jesus says, in John, "It is accomplished" (John 19:20).

His fulfillment of the Law, through his personally fulfilling the will of God, Jesus shares with Christians of every age. We can make our own the words of Paul and rejoice in our sufferings, and in our own flesh fill up what is lacking in the afflictions of Christ on behalf of his Body, which is the Church (see Col 1:24). Let us be careful not to build up again those things that Christ tore down (see Gal 2:18).

. . . I live by faith in the Son of God who has loved me and given himself for me" (Gal 2:20). J. I. González Faus says, "The concept of religion is enormously complicated. . . . Moreover, its application to Christianity is for me very questionable and in any case very derivative" (*Unicity of God, Multiplicity of Mysticisms*, CJ Booklet 147 [Barcelona: Cristianisme i justicia, 2013], 3). If Christianity is not a religion, that fact certainly has implications for the topic *religious freedom*.

14

On Matthew 6:1-8, 16-18

In chapter five of his Rule for Monasteries, Saint Benedict distinguishes between obedience and obedience. There is voluntary obedience and there is grumbling obedience.

Voluntary obedience is acceptable and sweet, but it is mostly characterized negatively as not being like grumbling obedience. So voluntary obedience is not anxious, it is not slow, and it is not half-hearted. It is non-complaining and is free from any hint of unwillingness. "If a disciple obeys grudgingly . . . , not only aloud but also in his heart, then even though he carries out the order, his action will not be accepted with favor by God who sees that he is grumbling in his heart. He will have no reward" (RB 5.14-19).

We see that voluntary obedience is not about the one who gives an order or makes a request, the abbot or whoever. It is not even about the thing that has been asked or commanded, which is often indifferent and could just as well be asked of someone else.

Rather, obedience is the monk's heart exercise; it is the irreplaceable opportunity for the monk to stop being held hostage to his ego and to start living more freely in the image of Christ.

Saint Benedict directs us to Second Corinthians chapter nine. There Paul quotes from Proverbs: "God loves a cheerful giver" (2 Cor 9:7; Prov 22:8 LXX). Benedictine voluntary obedience is not grumbling but cheerful, which is a quality of both the heart and the face.

In that same paragraph of his letter Paul gives God himself as the model of generosity: "He scatters abroad, he gives to the poor; his righteousness endures forever" (2 Cor 9:9; Ps 112:9). God's generosity in providential giving is his righteousness.

Righteousness is a godlike, religious quality that is expressed in a specific action, so that the action itself can be called a *righteousness*. It is this identification of the quality "righteousness" with a concrete deed that is behind Jesus' warning in the Sermon on the Mount "not to perform your righteousness before others just so they can see it" (Matt 6:1).

The New American Bible Revised Edition correctly translates *righteousness* in this verse as "righteous deeds." Jesus is about to identify three righteous deeds: almsgiving, prayer, and fasting. These are now the traditional Christian Lenten practices. In context, they are things that the blessed ones of the Beatitudes do, the poor in spirit, the clean of heart, and those who hunger and thirst for righteousness. These happy people are proactive and do the righteous thing themselves. These righteous deeds are actions that when we do them we are somehow imitating God.

Jesus introduces each of these righteous deeds in the same way: "When you . . . do not." That is, *when you* do them, *do not* be like the hypocrites. The difference is between being seen and not being seen. Jesus' true disciples, the blessed ones, do righteous deeds without drawing attention to themselves, not even their own attention: don't let your left hand know what your right is doing (Matt 6:3). False disciples, the hypocrites, do them for show and to get approval.

But this difference is very much like that one Benedict makes between obedience and obedience. Hypocritical obedience that is slow, complaining, and half-hearted is sure to draw attention to itself—a disgruntled look, throwing things, many visits to the abbot explaining why you can't do it, complaining to others about the injustice done you, self-righteously doing the minimum, and leaving things only partly finished so someone else has occasion to murmur against you.

Voluntary sweet obedience, by contrast, slides through in a flash unnoticed except for the attractive cheerfulness that accompanies it. There is nothing to say.

Another thing is that with each instance of righteousness God, who is "your Father," sees in secret and rewards you.

Saint Benedict says the same about voluntary obedience, only indirectly: if grumbling obedience "will have no reward" (RB 5.19), then voluntary obedience will have. As Saint Paul says about your generosity to others, God "will increase the harvest of your righteousness" (2 Cor 9:10).

For a long time I was uncomfortable about the idea of doing good works, deeds of righteousness, for a reward. It seemed mercenary and contractual—if you do that, then I give you this—and not consistent with unconditional Christian love, the self-giving love of the cross that does not count the cost.

But now I see that my attitude is just a form of spiritual pride and is probably Pelagian, a denial that I need any reward. It is forgetting what I just said Paul said, about God scattering abroad because his righteousness endures forever.

Paul ends that paragraph with a little paean to God's "indescribable free gift" (2 Cor 9:15). It is ultimately God who is the cheerful giver; he can't help it, and he loves opportunities to reward, even makes them if he has to. The rewards were already given with the Beatitudes: the kingdom of God, consolation, the vision of God. Who would refuse or turn them down on the basis of a do-it-yourself kind of piety?

In any case, Saint Bernard didn't share my scruples. He begins chapter seven of his little treatise *On Loving God* stating its theme: "Now let us consider what *profit* we shall have from loving God."[1]

Bernard will affirm that, yes, "Love is an affection of the soul, not a contract," so you would not *expect* a reward for love: "it is

---

1. This and what follows comes from Dil 17–22; see CF 13:109–15, *passim*.

the reluctant, not the eager, whom we urge by promises of reward. . . . No one would offer to pay a hungry man to eat."

Even more, says Bernard, if you love God in the hope of getting a reward, then what you really love is the reward and not God, who then is only the *apparent* object of desire.

Be that as it may, "He wills not to leave love unrewarded."

The reward of love is not a recompense owed but a function of the Beloved's good pleasure, of the will of him who is all Good. Love "has its reward, but the reward is the object that is loved. . . . One who loves God truly asks no other recompense than God himself."

We spoke of the deeds of righteousness and of the fact that when they are done in the secret of a pure heart out of love they are seen by the Father who sees in secret and gives a reward. But righteousness, as Bernard says, "can no more be satisfied by earthly treasures than the hungry body can be satisfied by air." "The motive" for deeds of righteousness, he goes on, for voluntary obedience without delay, for loving God, "is God himself. God is both the efficient cause and final object of our love. He gives the occasion for love, creates the affection, brings the desire to good effect. . . . Our love is prepared and rewarded by his . . . yet he has no gift better than himself. He gives him*self* as prize and reward."

For his part, Saint Aelred says that it is our "glory that, from the grace of our Lord, some merit of our own might lead the way to the fullness of blessing that the Creator's kindness would bestow upon us. Happiness itself is thus both a gift and a reward" (Oner 17.9, my translation; see CF 83:162).

15

On Matthew 6:7-8

(Luke 12:30)

Jesus assures us, "Your Father knows what you need before you ask him" (Matt 6:8). His topic is prayer. Our prayer—"ask him"—is the personal activity of one member of a relationship. The personal activity of the other member is God's knowledge—"your Father knows." Between the two activities, prayer and knowledge, is our need. Jesus gives this teaching by way of explaining what he had just said: in praying don't pile up empty phrases or use a lot of words (Matt 6:7).

But in Matt 6:8 there is another element of prayer to consider, and that is time. It is signaled by the word "before." God's knowledge of our need precedes our asking for *what* we need. God's knowledge comes before our prayer. There is nothing surprising here, for he chose us before the foundation of the world (Eph 1:4).

It is probably even the case that God knows what we need before we know what we need.

If I am honest, I have to say I am much more aware of what I want than of what I need, and what I think I need is usually really only what I want but do not need at all. This blurring of the boundary between wants and needs can explain things like eating disorders, for instance, and jealousy and resentment, getting to bed too late to get enough sleep, and why our conscience weighs us down.

God knows our needs. It is our needs that Jesus says our Father cares about, not our wants, unless we have gotten to that state of mature consciousness where our desires and our needs are the same, and then, as it turns out, our need and our desire are condensed in the One, the One Thing necessary, the One whom our soul loves and whom we seek in waking prayer and in sleeping dreams.[1]

Saint Bernard was talking to his monks about Jesus' curing the paralytic (Matt 9:1-7). Jesus told the paralytic, "Arise, take up your bed, and walk." Bernard's interpretation illustrates this point about needs and desires, and about needs and desires finally coming together in one act of prayer. In his interpretation we can understand "soul" as desire-for-the-Only-Need, and "body" as imagined needs and other things we want. "If you now arise with desire for heavenly realities," says Bernard,

> if you take up your bed, raising your *body* from earthly pleasures so that your *soul* is no longer carried by her concupiscence, but rather, as is proper, your *soul rules your body* and bears it to where it would not choose, eventually, if you walk *forgetting the things that are behind, and stretching forth to things that are before* [Phil 3:13] with the desire and intention of finally attaining them, then you need not doubt that you

1. See, for instance, Gregory the Great, Mor in Job 5.XXXVIII.68, where the angels overcome their natural mutability when, as it were, by their own free choice (*arbitrio*), they bind it by the chains of the love of God; and Dante's *Paradiso*, where Piccarda tells Dante "Brother, the virtue of Charity quiets our will, by making it desire only what we have and to thirst for nothing more. . . . Indeed, it is the very form of this blessed state to keep ourselves within the divine will, so that our wills are made one and the same" (III.70–72, 79–81). Eleonore Stump says, "If a person takes God as her deepest desire, all her other heart's desires . . . can refold, can reshape without losing their identity, by being woven into that deepest desire" (*Wandering in Darkness: Narrative and the Problem of Suffering* [Oxford: Clarendon, 2010], 445). Also, "It is possible for a person to lose the desires of his heart when they are inimical to his ultimate flourishing, but to gain them again in their refolded form when they are interwoven with a deepest desire for God" (Stump, *Wandering*, 464). See also #22, n. 1, below.

have been cured. For you would not be able to rise if you
had not been somewhat relieved of your burden, or to pick
up your bed unless you were at least in part unburdened.
(Div 25.4, emphases added; see CF 68:184)

In the same sermon, Bernard comments on chapter twenty of
the Rule of Saint Benedict, "On Reverence in Prayer." "I notice,"
he says, "that not a few of us sometimes experience a certain dry-
ness and dullness of mind in prayer, as though praying with the
lips only. That is because we don't pay attention; we come to prayer
out of habit, not carefully and with a suitable sense of awe (see
Div 25.7; CF 68:144–45).

But at the same time, maybe we need to be a little more forward
and bold when we pray than we suppose we should be. I mean, it
is true that we are sinners when we pray, and that fact might in-
spire some understandable reticence. But Bernard says that when
you pray to God, you should do it in the same way that a sick
person approaches a doctor.

Sick people know that they're sick and not too pleasant to be
around, but they also know that people in their condition are
exactly the kind of people doctors are there to receive with the
utmost attention (see Div 107.1; CF 68:391).

God is inclined to the sinner as doctors are to sick persons. So,
sure, we pray with a certain self-effacing modesty (*pudore*); we try
to be sincere (*puro*), big-hearted (*amplo*), and devout (*devoto*). But
Bernard does not hesitate to call us to pray directly to God—as
Moses did, with whom the Lord spoke "face to face as a person
speaks to a friend" (Exod 33:11; see Div 107.1; CF 68:391–92).

Even though "God is everywhere," says Bernard, let's imagine
him in heaven at the time of prayer, so that our mind, too, not
hindered by the roof of the chapel, nor by the intervening space
of the air, nor by the thickness of the clouds, is also in heaven with
him. This is what Jesus means when he tells us to pray, "Our Father
who art in heaven" (Matt 6:9). Let us pray "as though [we have]
been taken up and presented to God, who sits upon a throne high

among the angels." When you pray, be like one of those poor whom God lifted out of the dunghill (Ps 113:7; Div 25.8; see CF 68:145–46). Be as alert as someone standing before the Lord of majesty (see 1 Cor 2:8); say with Abraham, I may be dust and ashes, but still, I will speak to my Lord (see Gen 18:27).

Jesus himself, "in the days of his flesh," prayed with reverent awe (Heb 5:7). He took his own advice and did not use a lot of words, but prayed with "groans and tears." Even the Lord's Prayer, now an artfully crafted liturgical formula in the gospel of Matthew, was originally the single personal word "Abba," like a groan, onto which Jesus added the One Thing Necessary: "your will be done" (Mark 14:36).

I think that problems with prayer come from problems of faith. I don't mean faith in the church's dogmas and in the articles of the Creed; I mean the living personal faith that can move mountains, the faith that undergirds a friendship.

Paul's arguments about faith versus the Law are valid for all times and for every form of spirituality. We have problems with prayer and everything else, for that matter, when our spirituality is one of obligation, duty, accomplishment, prerequisites, and satisfying expectations, from whatever quarter they come to us.

Jesus' whole life was a preparation for and the continual practice of prayer. You can't reserve desire for the One Thing Necessary for twenty minutes a day and then spend the rest of your time with your mind and your will occupied somewhere else. Saint Aelred says that "those whose consciences rejoice in the memory of good works when they pray . . . raise themselves in a kind of confidence and offer themselves to the divine gaze" (Oner 5.11; CF 83:57).

Monastic practices and ascesis do nothing if they do not prepare us for and dispose us to prayer, so that we are intentionally praying at all times. What we choose to read, what we choose to talk about with someone, where we choose to be when we don't *have* to be somewhere, the content of our thoughts in silence and solitude—we cannot expect what we are at prayer to be different from what we are before prayer, and what we are after a prayer that is humble, reverent, and pure cannot but be the effect of the prayer itself.

Finally, in community, the prayerful dispositions of each brother or sister have an effect on all. Saint Aelred talks about the fervor that is *necessary* for a community of brothers gathered for the *opus Dei*: "This fervor leads to that interior fire spreading everywhere through the sound from the mouth. The brothers can thus raise one another up and light a spark in one another, until one flame springs from the many" (Oner 5.10; CF 83:57).

16

On Matthew 6:9

(Mark 14:35-36; Luke 11:1-2)

"Pray, then, like this, 'Our Father'" (Matt 6:5, 9).

Jesus gave his disciples a prayer, the Lord's Prayer, and ever since it has identified the disciples of Jesus of Nazareth.

In his letters to the Galatians and to the Romans Saint Paul talks about Christians praying "Abba, Father" (Gal 4:6; Rom 8:15). Paul introduces this prayer easily. He doesn't have to explain this formula of prayer. He knows that his Christian audience will understand. "When you pray, say, 'Abba, Father!'"

Paul is referring to the Lord's Prayer, which any catechized Christian then as now would know and love.

We get another look at Jesus' prayer in chapter eleven of Matthew: "At that time Jesus said, 'I give praise to you Father, Lord of heaven and earth, for although you have hidden these things from the wise and the learned, you have revealed them to the childlike'" (Matt 11:25).

Matthew says Jesus prayed this prayer of thanksgiving "at that time." It was the first century of the present era.

> Where are your wonders of old? How long will you forget us?
>   Forever?
> *Have you noticed my servant Job?*

In first-century Palestine people were wondering when—or if—the old prophecies would ever be fulfilled.

John the Baptist wondered about that. In prison, John had just sent disciples to Jesus asking if Jesus was really "the coming one." Jesus sent them back with prophet's words—"the poor have good news preached to them"—and added his own beatitude for John: "Blessed is he who takes no offense at me" (Matt 11:2-6; Isa 61:1).

It was at *that* time that Jesus said, "I thank you, Father . . . for you have . . . revealed these things to the childlike," and added, "Come to me . . . and you will find rest for yourselves" (Matt 11:28, 29).

People remembered that once the Lord God had said to King David through the prophet Nathan, "I will raise up your offspring after you . . . and I will establish his kingdom . . . forever. He it is who will build a house to my name. . . . I will be a father to him, and he will be a son to me" (2 Sam 7:12-14).

This was one of those prophecies that people were waiting to be fulfilled. It was a prophecy that kept the hope alive for the coming of the Messiah, the King. The son it talked about and the house he would build where the *Father's name* would dwell and be praised were signs that the *kingdom* had drawn near, *had come* at last.

Jesus knew that he was that son.

Certainly, his family would not have hidden from Jesus what Matthew wrote for the whole world, that Jesus was "the son of David"; he was "Emmanuel" promised by the prophet Isaiah who would "save his people from their sins." His very person accomplished what the Temple and the Temple's liturgy aspired to: the glorification of the name of the Lord (Matt 1:1, 33, 21).

Most of all, Jesus had heard a voice from heaven: "This is my beloved Son" (Matt 3:17). He called the one who spoke, "My Father," "Abba."

When he gave us his prayer, the Lord's Prayer, Jesus was announcing that the kingdom was near, and so not far, and that the prophecies of the past were Good News for the present and future.

He also gave us his breath and his life. He made *us* children of his, and our, Father in heaven (see Matt 5:45).

> Isaac was father Abraham's beloved son.
> *Yes; as you are mine; and it's still true that God will provide the sheep for the holocaust; and, as you put it, the time for that is at hand.*

The Lord's Prayer opens with the invocation, "Our Father who art in heaven" (Matt 6:9). Is heaven, then, a place that you can *be in*?

However you answer that, one thing we can affirm for certain is that for the Bible heaven is a point of departure. The Lord said to Moses, "I have witnessed the affliction of my people . . . I have heard their cry . . . I know well what they are suffering. Therefore, I have come down to rescue them" (Exod 3:7-8). Heaven is the place he comes from.

Take, for example, the psalm in the Book of the Prophet Isaiah, chapters sixty-three and sixty-four. It was written during the Babylonian Exile. It is clear that the memory of the destruction of the Temple in Jerusalem is still fresh to the prophet. The psalm is an appeal to God. At the very center of the poem is what is in my opinion one of the most exquisite verses of biblical poetry:

> *Oh, that you would rend the* heavens
> *and come down;*

and it continues:

> *Then your* name *would be known to your enemies . . .*
> *while you worked awesome deeds we could not hope for.*
> (Isa 63:19–64:2)

This poem by Isaiah begins by recalling God's deeds, the abundance of his acts of faithful love to his people. God says through the prophet, "Truly they are my people, children who will not betray me" (Isa 63:8).

But now it is the Exile; now, the prophet wonders, "Where is he who saved them from the sea, the Shepherd of his flock?" (Isa 63:11). The poem continues with the supplication, addressed, we notice, to God as Father:

> *Look down from* heaven *and regard us*
> *from your holy and glorious palace.* . . .
> *Where is your zealous care* . . .
> *your surge of pity?*
> *Your mercy hold not back.* . . .
> *You, Lord, are* our Father,
> *"Our Redeemer" you are named from of old.* . . .
> *Oh, that you would rend the* heavens *open and come down.* . . .
> *For you have hidden your face from us.* . . .
> *Yet, Lord, you are* our Father;
> *we are the clay and you our potter,*
> *we are all the work of your hand.* (Isa 63:16–64:8, emphasis mine)

It is all of this, these memories and hopes, threats, complaints and lamentations, that Jesus summed up with the limpid invocation, "Our Father who art in heaven."

But, again, just what is this heaven that the Father is in, that the prophet implored be rent?

We can start with our recent experiences of extreme weather.[1] Heaven is a complex of uncontrollable powers that affect what happens on earth. It is a domain not accessible to human measurement or to human manipulation.

In other words, heaven is like God. The psalmist says it best: "Our God is in the heavens; he does whatever he wills" (Ps 115:3). Heaven is inaccessible to us, but it exercises a determinative and even definitive influence on life here and now.

---

1. For this brief treatment of heaven see Michael Welker, *God the Spirit* (Minneapolis: Fortress, 1994), 137–42.

In the Bible heaven is not only spatial but also temporal. As temporal, it is not only the present; it is the past, too, and the transcendence that lies temporally before us: heaven is the future.

Those forces that in our earthly experience clearly diverge and are separated in space and time, heaven brings together. Heaven is a field of reference that extends beyond peoples, cultures, climates, and times, and in that way it also unites them.

Though creatures and regions, events and times, be separate from one another, still, they all have in common the fact that they live under what relative to human mortality is the eternal heaven with its stars and their attendant orders and rhythms.

So to answer the question we began with, heaven is rightly the place of the presence of God. In heaven is where our Father is.

Being there, our Father is everywhere and immediate to all.

Furthermore, it is because our Father is in heaven that he is our Father, and not yours or mine alone.

In the Book of Job we find this. It is Eliphaz speaking, one of Job's friends. He is a false witness, putting into Job's mouth words that Job had never said:

> *Does not God, in the heights of the heavens,*
> *behold the top of the stars, high though they are?*
> *Yet you say, "What does God know?*
> *Can he judge through the thick darkness?*
> *Clouds hide him so that he cannot see,*
> *as he walks aroung the circuit of the heavens." (Job 22:12-14)*

Eliphaz would have us believe that heaven is God's hiding place, transcendence for the sake of indifference, Old Yahweh in self-imposed angry exile.

The truth of the matter is the other way round:

> *In my distress I called out: Lord!*
> *I cried out to my God.*
> *He parted the heavens and came down.*

Who is like the Lord our God,
   enthroned on high,
   looking down on heaven and earth?
He raises the needy from the dust. (Pss 18:7, 10; 113:5-7)

The entire Bible, the single great sweeping story it tells over and over again, ends with "the New Jerusalem coming down out of heaven from God" (Rev 21:10). God comes to save his people.

Heaven is where he comes from and at the same time never leaves, then, and now, and in the millennium fast unfolding. So now, as much as ever, we have the courage and faith to say, "Our Father, who art in heaven."

17

On Matthew 6:9-10

(Luke 11:2; see John 12:28)

In the Lord's Prayer, Jesus shows concern for his Father's reputation, his Father's good name. "Hallowed be thy name" is the first of the Prayer's petitions.

In the book of Malachi, the Lord says to his people, not without irony and bitterness, "Incense offerings are made to my name *everywhere*, for my name is great among the nations. . . . But *you* profane it" (Mal 1:11-12; emphasis mine), as if to say, "All the nonbelievers honor me in spite of themselves, but you, my very own people, say, 'Profaned be God's Name,'" a clear violation of the second commandment (see Exod 20:7).

How were the people in exile profaning God's name? In the view of the prophets, the exile in Babylon itself was the profanation of the Lord's holy name. According to the logic of the prophets, granted that the *cause* of the exile was the people's sin, the *fact* of the exile itself tarnished the Lord's reputation, cast a bad light upon his great name.

But still, how could God's name be profaned by a population of political refugees and deportees?

No one drove this point home better than Ezekiel. In Ezekiel 36 the name of the Lord appears as a personal being capable of suffering.[1]

---

1. See Walther Zimmerli, *Ezekiel II: A Commentary on the Book of the Prophet Ezekiel Chapters 25–48* (Minneapolis: Fortress, 1983), 246.

It is this text of Ezekiel more than any other that stands behind the first petition of the Lord's Prayer, "Hallowed be thy name."

Ezekiel writes, *Son of man, . . . when [the House of Israel] came to the nations . . . they desecrated my holy name, for people said, "These are the people of the Lord, yet they had to leave their land"* (Ezek 36:17-21).

Ezekiel's point is that those Israelite exiles, precisely through their dispersion, robbed the Lord's holy name of its holiness and profaned it. Their exile caused the nations to doubt the Lord's professed fidelity, the Lord's love, the Lord's power to deliver, with respect to those he had named "my people."

The Lord's name, which is his very person, was profaned, desecrated, "de-hallowed" among the nations, because the dispersed People of God were living like sheep without a shepherd.

When Jesus teaches us to pray "Hallowed be thy name," he is recalling Ezekiel's text and declaring its definitive reversal. In fact, in Ezekiel 36 the Lord himself maps out the method of reparation: *Now* I *will show* the holiness of my great name. . . . *I will take you away from among the nations . . . and bring you back to your own soil. I will sprinkle clean water over you. . . . I will give you a new heart . . . . I will put my spirit within you. . . . You will be my people and I will be your God* (Ezek 36:23, 24, 25, 26, 27, 28; emphasis mine).

With the Lord's Prayer, God is "Our Father," whose name we hallow by allowing him to deliver us from the evil one. This is nothing less than the end of the exile and the restoration of the Father's reputation. It is the coming of the kingdom of God. It is what we pray for and at the same time proclaim when we say, "Hallowed be thy name." It is the Lord's fidelity to himself in being faithful to us, for his sake and ours.

But it calls for a response of fidelity on our part. We pray that the Father's name be hallowed "on earth as it is in heaven." There is no question that God's name is hallowed in heaven. The case is different in the random and seemingly capricious flow of history on earth. Exile from heaven and profanation of the holy name are still always possibilities.

As if anticipating those possibilities, at the end of Mass the deacon or the priest sends us off with a challenge that echoes the second petition of the Lord's Prayer: "Go in peace, glorifying the Lord by your life."

Taking the noun *glory* to mean inherent excellence, there's no question that we can do anything to add to God's glory. We do not glorify the Lord by somehow enhancing his intrinsic excellence.

But glory also means a good reputation. We can do a lot to glorify God in this sense. How we live can help give God a good name. The deacon, then, is repeating what Jesus said: let people see your good works so they will "glorify your heavenly Father" (Matt 5:16). Our behavior as Christians redounds to God's good name.

With the disciples to whom Jesus addressed himself we constitute the People of God. In Jesus, we are the chosen, the first-born son, and in us is our Father glorified, his name held holy. Our very lives become the heavenly liturgy upon earth, our personal actions done in secret as well as our corporate acts as the visible church.

Our very bodies, our individual bodies in their odd shapes and misshapes, our communal body in worship of the Father and in mutual service of our brothers and sisters, our very body is a Temple of the Holy Spirit within us. We are not our own, says Saint Paul; we were bought with a price. So let us glorify God, hallow his name, in our body (see 1 Cor 6:19-20).

18

On Matthew 6:11-12 I

The last four petitions of the Lord's Prayer come in two pairs, Matthew 6:11-12 and Matthew 6:13. In this talk and the next one we'll consider the first pair. In #20 and #21 we'll consider the second pair.

The two members of the first pair (the fourth and fifth petitions, about bread and forgiveness) are joined by the linking word *and*: "give us this day our daily bread and forgive us our trespasses, as we forgive those who trespass against us" (Matt 6:11-12).

The *and* that comes between the two petitions tells us that the two petitions somehow go together. The *and* signals that the second member is an intensification or concrete example of what is said in the first, something like "Of course your daughter can stay with us during your recovery, and she will have her own bedroom." Our need for bread, and our need to forgive and be forgiven, are companion needs.

Let us look at the bread need first, "Give us this day our daily bread."

In the Greek text of Matthew, all of the words are familiar and intelligible, except for one. The unusual word is the one that we translate as "daily." The Greek word is *epiousion*, and to translate it as *daily* is just a guess.

When you think of it, even in English it doesn't make much sense: what is "daily bread?" Is it a kind of bread, like whole wheat and sourdough? If you own a bakery, maybe you bake bread daily;

maybe you even have a daily quota of bread to bake, but you probably don't talk about baking daily bread. What does *daily* really add to the petition?

Long ago, the church father Origen pointed out that the word we translate as *daily* is not found anywhere else in the entire Bible or even in Greek literature outside the Bible. People didn't even use it in day-to-day conversations. Ever since then, scholars and commentators have puzzled over this word.[1]

Origen concluded that *epiousion* was an invention of the evangelists, and his judgment is still as good as any, but as far as I can tell, no one has taken seriously the obvious implication of what Origen pointed out seventeen hundred years ago. If it is true that *epiousion* is a brand new word never seen before, so that no one knows what it means—then that's the whole key to its meaning.

When you come to the phrase "*epiousion* bread" you have to ask, "What kind of bread is that?"

When you ask that question, immediately you're one of the Israelites in the wilderness journeying from slavery to freedom and saying to one another, "What is that?" To which question Moses responds, "That is the bread that the Lord has given you to eat" (Exod 16:15).[2]

The Bread of the Lord's Prayer is something given us uniquely by our Father.

Bread shows up in the gospel of Matthew other times besides in the Lord's Prayer. Jesus reminds the devil that real human life is nourished not just by bread but by what comes from the mouth of God; just as a father will not give his child a stone when he needs bread, so our heavenly Father will give us good things when we ask him; on two occasions, Jesus satisfies the hunger of huge crowds with a very small quantity of bread; there is children's bread whose crumbs are powerful to save; there is a bread that is the object of belief and understanding; finally, there is the bread that

---

1. See almost any critical commentary on the gospel of Matthew.
2. In Deut 8:3 it is called *manna* from the Hebrew *man hu*, "What is it?"

is My Body, given, for you to take and eat (Matt 4:3; 7:9; 14:17-19; 15:33-38; 15:26; 15:5-12; 26:26).

It would be strange, then, if the bread of the Lord's Prayer alone of all the other breads in Matthew were merely water and wheat. It would be strange if it alone were not the same as they: miraculous, gracious, unattainable, necessary, given, life-giving, memorable, and enduring.

We have seen all the occurrences of bread in the gospel of Matthew, except for one. Let's look at that one now (see Matt 12:1-8).

Jesus and his disciples are walking through grain fields on the Sabbath. When the disciples begin to pick and eat some grain, Jesus speaks up and defends them against the accusation that they are breaking the Sabbath. His defense rests on what David and his own followers did in 1 Samuel 21:1-6, when they were a band of hungry outlaws: they went into the house of God and ate the loaves of bread offered to God, bread that only the priests were permitted to eat.

Jesus concludes by affirming that right there in that grain field, because he is there, there is something greater than the house of God and, further, that he himself is Lord of the Sabbath, meaning the one who inhabits the house of God.

As a consequence, Jesus reframes the whole scene in the light of God's own *chesed*, divine loving-kindness, and quotes the prophet Hosea to make the point: *Mercy [chesed] I desire, and not sacrifice* (see Hos 6:6).

In this scene in the grainfield, Jesus is the priest whose holocaust is his own loving-kindness; Jesus is both the Temple and the Temple's bread of presence. Jesus is the Torah's Lord, its origin and its fulfillment. He is David, the anointed king, and with his band of followers the beginning of a God-sanctioned revolution. To be in fellowship with Jesus in a field of grain is to be a guest in the dining room of the King; even if the meal is only raw grain, or morsels of unleavened bread, it is a banquet of rich food and fine wines, given free, communicating to the guests the compassion of their host (see Isa 25:6).

It is all of these breads, along with Jesus who is both meal and host, that we have in mind when we pray, "Father, give us this day our daily bread."

When we pray for our "daily bread" it is right to think of the Eucharist. But it would not be wrong to do the reverse: when we receive the Eucharist, to remember the bread in its abundant manifestations and marvelous revelations.

What is it? The food of mercy, the bread of ministry, the necessary nurturing that the Father is pleased to give his children:

> You have given them the bread of angels.
> *I have made them little less than gods.*
> You have given me the bread of understanding, the water of
>   wisdom.
> *Your bread will be ashes, your drink mingled with tears.*

19

On Matthew 6:11-12 II

The fifth petition of the Lord's Prayer is "and forgive us our trespasses as we forgive those who trespass against us" (Matt 6:12).

The *and* at the beginning connects this petition in a positive way to the one before it about daily Bread (#18). The petition asks that the gift of the Bread be followed by forgiveness, which itself is also always a gift.

This is the only petition in the Lord's Prayer that has two members, a request followed by what looks like a condition. It is also the only petition that comes close to making an unconditional statement, "we forgive." In this petition, different from the others, the ones praying, "we" are almost self-consciously present, more so than in any of the other petitions. Nearly one-third of the total number of words in this petition refer to "us."

Finally, it is only in this petition that "we" are like "our Father," or, perhaps better stated, that our Father is like us. We both do the same thing; both of us are beings who forgive. There is something luminous and tremendous here.

Long-standing English-language biblical and liturgical traditions have translated the Greek word *opheilēmata* as "trespasses" and the Greek word *opheiletais* as "those who trespass."

But both Greek words come from a verb that means *to owe* or *to be in debt*. Jesus uses language from the world of contractual economics to talk about forgiveness. He uses the metaphor of debt to talk about forgiveness of sins and of sinners.

One reason that he uses this metaphor, I think, is because trespasses can be rationalized away—it was a mistake; I didn't see the sign—but not debts. The bookkeeper can call up your debts from the database, and can pull from your file charge slips and loan agreements with your signature that cannot be denied. There is hard evidence for debts.

When the debt is so great that you cannot pay it back there are only two ways out, setting aside murder and suicide: you can declare bankruptcy, or you can ask your creditor to cancel the debt outright. And if the debt has been justly incurred, then choosing bankruptcy is cowardly.

That leaves only the plea for remission.

In the context of Matthew's gospel and of the Sermon on the Mount, to plead for remission is to ask for mercy, and that is what the fifth petition is: "O Father, cancel our debts, as we cancel those of our debtors."

According to the prayer, we understand that this last-minute plea for mercy is at the same time a commitment on our part to extend to fellow humans the mercy we hope to receive. Saint Benedict wants his monks to say the Lord's Prayer together twice a day just so they will say this petition together. He calls it a *marriage agreement* (*sponsio*; RB 13.13).

The *as* in the fifth petition of the Lord's Prayer makes it look as though our Father is supposed to model his forgiveness on our forgiveness of one another, as if our prior forgiving of others were a condition making a claim on God's forgiving us: "Forgive us *as we* forgive."

But to see it like that just shows that we are not yet convinced about either who we are when we pray this prayer or to whom it is that we pray.

In praying this Prayer of the Lord we recognize ourselves as children of the Father. When we pray the Lord's Prayer, we acknowledge that we have already received the "daily" Bread of Mercy. We are in the force field of our forgiving God.

The mistake is to hear chronology when in fact this odd two-part petition is organic.

What this petition means I will suggest by a kind of paraphrase: "Father, we want that the bread of your unexpected kingdom-mercy to us be broken and shared in the way that we freely mercy one another": "Forgive us our sins, in the way of us forgiving one another."[1]

---

1. See Sebastian Moore, *The Crucified Jesus Is No Stranger* (New York: Seabury, 1977), 88, 90.

20

On Matthew 6:13 I

(see John 17:13-15; Mark 14:37-48; Luke 22:39-46)

"Lead us not into temptation, but deliver us from the Evil One" (Matt 6:13). Once again we have a pair of petitions (see Matt 6:11-12).

Not only do these two petitions belong together and explain one another, but they also bring us right back to the beginning of the Prayer and make us understand everything we have just said.

The Prayer begins with the confident address "Father," but it ends with the dark menace of the "Evil One." And it goes on to describe what the kingdom of God on earth would be like, and ends with the very real possibility of our losing it all in apostasy, a prospect all the more disconcerting when we have to admit, besides, that it's in the hands of the very Father we are praying to to bring us, or not, to the place where we might fall.

"Lead us not into temptation." The Greek word we translate as *temptation* means in most cases a test or a trial. In the Old Testament, God puts people to the test to find out what his servants are really made of, the quality of their sincerity, the purity of their faith, the extent of their moral stamina.[1]

---

1. See Ceslas Spicq, *Theological Lexicon of the New Testament*, vol. 3 (Peabody, MA: Hendrickson, 1994), 80–90.

In the Old Testament Wisdom literature, the question is asked, *Qui tentatus non est, qualis sit?* "If you're not tested, what are you worth?" (Sir 34:11 Vulg).

The word is found in the story of Abraham: "God put Abraham to the test" (Gen 22:1). And in the wilderness of Sinai, when the people were afraid, Moses said to them, "Do not be afraid, for God has come only to test you, and put the fear of him upon you so you do not sin" (Exod 20:20).

For the Old Testament, then, testing, or "temptation," is a basic element of God's pedagogy: you learn to be smart only through trouble.[2]

In the New Testament, too, temptation can be given a positive valuation.

The Letter of James utters a beatitude over someone who "perseveres in temptation, for when he has been proven, he will receive the crown of life that [God] has promised to those who love him"—"Blessed" is that one (Jas 1:12).

Furthermore, in the Bible the result of the test is always something positive for the ones tested. Consider Abraham, the people in the desert, the student of Ben Sirach, and the one James is talking about who wears the crown of life. They all gain something essential through the test that would not have been possible without it.

But if that is the case, we are startled when Jesus teaches his followers to pray, "Lead us *not* into temptation," "*Don't* make us

2. See, for instance, Eleonore Stump's discussion of Saint Thomas Aquinas's view of the role of suffering (Eleonore Stump, *Wandering in Darkness: Narrative and the Problem of Suffering* [Oxford: Clarendon, 2010], 398–400). She quotes Thomas: "Now it sometimes happens that God hearkens not to a person's pleas but rather to his advantage. . . . God does not remove tribulations from the person stuck in them, even though he prays earnestly for God to do so, because God knows these tribulations help him forward to final salvation. And so although God truly does hearken, the person stuck in afflictions believes that God hasn't hearkened to him" (Saint Thomas Aquinas, *Expositio super Iob* 7.1, Stump's translation at 399).

be tested," as if he didn't get it that God's testing is always for our well-being.

There is nothing in the Old Testament like this petition.

Neither is there anything else like it in the Lord's Prayer itself, where this is the only negative petition.

The petition implies several things. First, that there is a test that it would not be good for us to take—better stay home from school that day. Second, that the very Father we are praying to is the one who can both put us in the testing situation and keep us from it. Third, that the testing situation is a kind of place.

We know that it is a kind of place because of the verb that is used: "*to lead into,*" or, better, to bring into, to make someone enter into. It is a verb of motion toward some place.

Whenever this verb is used in the Septuagint, the Greek version of the Old Testament (twenty-nine times), the destination in view is a physical place, for instance, the Temple, a house, a cave, a city, a bed chamber, even fetters into which feet are made to enter. Never is the destination something abstract like "a trial," or "a temptation," or an emotional state.

So the use of this verb in the Lord's Prayer would be unusual in terms of biblical precedent, unless Jesus meant the "test" as a place of some kind.

I bring this up because in the Lord's Prayer there are only two verbs of motion.

One is this one, "to bring into." The other is in the second petition, "come," "Thy Kingdom come." The verb "come" implies a place of departure and also a place of arrival, the destination of the coming. In that case, the place of arrival is our "earth."

What we need to say about the petition "Lead us not into temptation," then, is that it is not talking about something like a temptation to fudge on your resolve not to eat candy bars between meals during Lent, or to waste time on the Internet. The test we pray not to be led into in the Lord's Prayer is a trial in a category all its own. It has the physicality of geography and the finality of an arrival. We will return to this petition after considering its companion.

"But deliver us from the Evil One" (Matt 6:13). The *but* joins this petition with the one that went before, about leading into temptation. The *but* tells us that the petition that follows it is saying the same thing as the one that went before it, reducing any doubt about what is intended. You might tell the barista who is about to pour milk in your coffee, "No milk; just the coffee, but black and strong."

In most English-language versions this petition is "but deliver us from evil." But there are good reasons for understanding the petition to be referring not to general evil, but to a personal being, Satan or the Devil—the Evil One; the Greek word Matthew uses can be translated either way, depending on the context.

For instance, in Jesus' parable of the sower and the seed, it is not "evil" but the "Evil One" who snatches the word of the kingdom from the heart of the person who has heard it (Matt 13:19).

In the rest of Matthew, the word *evil* is almost always an adjective describing humans, a use that wouldn't make sense in the Lord's Prayer.

In addition, in his account of Jesus' forty days in the wilderness, Matthew uses two of the key words in Matthew 6:13: the Spirit *leads* Jesus *into* the desert to be *tempted*. Jesus' opponent there is the Devil, also called the Tempter/Tester and Satan (Matt 4:1, 3, 10).

So the petition "but deliver us from evil" refers to something much more threatening than a general metaphysical evil. It is the Evil One, the Devil and Satan.

In any case, we don't have to make a hard and fast distinction between the Evil One and just plain evil; where you find one, you'll find the other: in Jesus' view, the one and the other are the real enemy.

The word translated *deliver* is relatively rare in the New Testament. It is used only 17 times (compared to the 107 occurrences of another word for *deliver* in the sense of *save*), and only 3 times in the gospels, twice in Matthew and once in Luke.

Neither is it common in the Greek version of the Old Testament. Noteworthy, then, is its fairly strong presence in the Greek version of the second and third parts of the prophet Isaiah.[3] There the Lord describes himself as "Your *Deliverer*, the Holy One of Israel," and the people say, "You, Lord, are our *Father*, 'Our *Deliverer*' is your *name* from of old. . . . Oh, that you would rend the heavens and come down,"[4] a text we have heard before (#16).

I don't think we need press this too far, but with the word *deliver*, too, there is a suggestion of movement, from a place of danger to a place of safety, even a violent tearing or dragging away,[5] as you might do in a desperate attempt to rescue your child from a savage attacker, or a beloved Son from a cross. So Saint Paul uses this word *deliver* in Colossians, "[God] has *delivered* us from *the power of darkness* and transferred us *to the kingdom* of his beloved Son" (Col 1:13).

3. See, e.g., Isa 44:6; 47:4; 49:7, 26; 50:2; 54:5, 8; 59:20.

4. Isa 49:7; 63:16, 19.

5. See Bailly abr. 1919, ῥυομαι, tirer d'un danger (at https://outils.biblissima .fr/en/eulexis-web/); see also Raymond E. Brown, *New Testament Essays* (Milwaukee: Bruce, 1965), 252 and n. 113.

21

On Matthew 6:13 II

When we put the two petitions of Matthew 6:13 together, we notice several similarities between them. For one thing, the two petitions have the same word order. Second, in both of them the subject of the verb is God our Father, and the object of the verb is us. Third, the phrase "deliver from" in the second petition is just a positive way of saying "do not lead into" in the first.

These similarities tell us that Jesus is using the literary technique of parallelism. Since each of these elements in one of the petitions finds a partner in the other, the law of parallelism says that the remaining two elements are partners too.

If they are, then we can say that the "trial" we pray *not to be led into* is the realm of "the Evil One" *from* whom we pray *to be delivered*. The *test* we ask to be delivered from is *Satan's reign* upon the earth.

So the Prayer ends where it began, only backwards.

If the Prayer began with "Father," it ends with "the Evil One," the complete inversion of Abba Father. It ends with our admitting that a real possibility is our Father's leading us into the testing situation, as if the testing situation is a place that is the complete inversion of the kingdom that we have just prayed might come.

The last two petitions say the same thing; they make us acknowledge the real possibility of the kingdom of darkness reigning upon the earth, instead of the kingdom of the Father and the kingdom of light.

For those who have heard Jesus and allowed his word to take root in their hearts, who have left everything to follow him, giving him their trust and allegiance—for them, life without the kingdom of the Father would be a trial they could not endure.

It is a chilling scenario that must be taken into account, given the theological necessity of God's being free to do whatever he wills, and the fact of God-given human free will.

And isn't this possibility what is behind Jesus' question as recorded by the evangelist Saint Luke, "But when the Son of Man comes will he find faith on the earth?" (Luke 18:8)?

We can illustrate with the example of martyrs what it means that the test we pray to be delivered from is a world devoid of the kingdom of God.

Imagine three worlds. The first is the world where the kingdom of God will be in full actualization, truly "as in heaven, so also on earth." In that age to come, there will be no martyrs, or, to put it another way, in that age to come every person will be a martyr, every snowflake and stone shimmering with light and a witness to the marvelous achievement of God.

The second world is the time when the kingdom of God, generously sown, is still growing among the tares (see Matt 13:24-30). It is the world of the Church Militant, to use a venerable phrase. In that world, which is the one we live in, martyrdom is as natural as sunrise. To those with eyes to see, martyrs today are irrefutable signs of the presence and vitality of the kingdom of their Father. Far from being a trial, martyrdom is the inevitable vocation of every Christian and is the assurance of things hoped for, the conviction of things not seen (see Heb 11:1).

You have already guessed the third scenario. It is a world where the seed of the Word has been thoroughly uprooted from hearts, a world where God no longer hears the plea "Your kingdom come," because there is no one on earth moved to pray it, a world where there is no trace of the kingdom of God, but in its place the rule of the Evil One.

In such a world as this last one, there would be no martyrs at all, no witnesses, no miracles of hymns coming from the mouths of mutilated, half-dead Christian children; stones and snowflakes would be only cold and silent.

It is this third scenario, this world without martyrs, that is the world we pray not to be led into; it is the trial we ask to be delivered from.[1]

Two of the principal words of this double petition concluding the Lord's Prayer show up only once more in Matthew's gospel, both in the context of Jesus' passion. One of them is the word for temptation or trial; the other is the word for deliver.

1. *Trial* in the context of Jesus' passion:

In Gethsemane on the night of his arrest, Jesus says to Peter and the sons of Zebedee, "Watch and pray that you may not enter into [the] *trial*" (Matt 26:41). This is after Jesus' first prayer to his Father that the cup might pass him by. Jesus is asking his disciples to pray along with him that the *Father's will be done*; to pray that his way of accomplishing that will, a way astoundingly clear to him, will achieve the end desired by the Father. "Watch and pray that you many not enter into [the] *trial*."

The phrase "not enter into" makes us think of "lead us not into," and suggests a movement toward something, as if the trial were a place, a realm, or an atmosphere.

In Gethsemane Jesus knows that he himself will *enter into* that place alone, one man (*hen anthrōpos*) for all, as Paul says (see Rom 5).[2] He knows that by entering into that trial himself, as one

---

1. The "third scenario" could also be called "hell," which Eleonore Stump says is "the worst thing that could happen to a human being." "To be in this condition," she says, "is to be everlastingly at a distance from oneself, from all other persons, and from God. It is to be endlessly isolated from God's redemptive goodness in self-willed loneliness." It is, she says, a "full-blown horror" (Eleonore Stump, *Wandering in Darkness: Narrative and the Problem of Suffering* [Oxford: Clarendon, 2010], 387).

2. See Rom 5:12-16. Paul's argument here is fundamental to the theology of the incarnation and redemption. He contrasts Adam and Jesus Christ, two "men" (*anthrōpoi*, the point being their humanity, not their maleness), and the effects of their respective choices and actions as "men" on "all men" (*pantes anthrōpoi*, that is, all human creatures, not all males only). In orthodox Christology, Jesus

entering "a strong man's house to bind him and plunder his goods" (Matt 12:29), he will make it unnecessary for his brothers and sisters to have to enter in.

He is about to enter the third world I described above. It is the realm of the absence of the Father, of the apparent victory of the Evil One, when the prophet from Nazareth will be unmasked before the world. Jesus told the disciples, then "My soul is very sorrowful, even to death" (Matt 26:38).

2. *Deliver* in the context of Jesus' passion:

The next day, on Calvary, the officials will mock Jesus: "Let him come down from the cross, and we will believe him. He trusts in God; let God *deliver* him now, if he desires him" (Matt 27:42, 43). At the ninth hour, Jesus cried with a loud voice, "My God, my God, why hast thou forsaken me?" (Matt 27:46).

The Prayer Jesus gives us to pray ends with us looking into this realm of the Evil One as still a real possibility. He hopes we will find the vision so intolerable that we will rush back to the beginning. He hopes that we will pray with greater understanding, and with more intense solidarity with our brothers and sisters, "Father, *your* kingdom come, *your* will be done, on earth, as it is in heaven."

Christ is a single divine "person" with two natures, a divine nature and a human nature. Paul's whole argument turns on this fact: it is what Jesus Christ did in his human nature that Paul contrasts to what Adam did in that same human nature. The playing field is even. Paul does not contrast the agency of the divine personhood of Jesus Christ with that of the human personhood of Adam, where the playing fields do not even touch. In Romans 5 Paul is talking about two "men," not about two "persons." Yet the NABRE translates each occurrence of *anthrōpos* in this passage from Romans, whether in reference to Jesus Christ or to Adam, as "person," making Paul a classical Docetist. The Letter to the Hebrews makes the same point in a dozen words as Paul in Romans 5 does in as many verses: "Now since the children share in blood and flesh, he [Christ] likewise shared in them, that through death he might destroy the one who has the power of death, that is, the devil"; "he had to become like his brothers in every way" (Heb 2:14, 17; see #33).

We understand now that *Your kingdom coming* is at least this: *Your delivering us from the kingdom of the Evil One.*

Nevertheless, the Prayer, as often as we pray it, keeps ending with the trial and the Evil One. They persist and do not go away. Are they just reminders of something that could have been? Are they warnings of something that still could be?

They are at least reminders of what Jesus has done for us, out of his very great love (see John 15:13; Gal 2:20).

22

On Matthew 6:20-21

When is the last time you used the word *treasure*? What was the context? Was it *treasure* as a noun, or *treasure* as a verb? What was the *treasure*, or what was it that you *treasured*?

I don't remember the last time I used the word *treasure*, but when I do use it, it is almost always the verb, not the noun. I say, "I treasure our friendship," but not "our friendship is a treasure," or "I treasure Sunday afternoons in the monastery," not "Sunday afternoons are my treasure."

When I say I *treasure* something I mean that I hold the person or the thing dear or precious, and that in a personal way, not in an objective, quantitative way.

So I don't expect that everyone else treasures a friendship with you or that every monk treasures Sunday afternoons in the monastery; some find Sunday afternoons a drag. What I treasure is something personally meaningful and valuable, and not necessarily meaningful and valuable in itself. One person's treasure is another person's trash, you might say.[1]

---

1. Eleonore Stump points out that human beings naturally set their hearts on things that may or may not be necessary for our ultimate flourishing (i.e., union in love with God). She calls these the "desires of the heart." But our ultimate flourishing "requires that [we] care about and seek to have things besides those that are intrinsically valuable components of or means to human flourishing. . . . [H]uman flourishing is not possible in the absence of the desires of the heart"

I don't claim any material thing to be a treasure. I like the guitar I have to use, but I don't consider that guitar my treasure. I wouldn't even consider a lot of cash in our checking account a treasure. I wouldn't say I *treasured* the fact that we were in the black; I would be grateful that we were because it would allow for helping others in meaningful ways and would preclude a lot of worries, but I wouldn't say I treasured our checking account in the way I say I treasure our friendship.

The verb *treasure* has another meaning. It does not mean only to prize or regard as precious and valuable; it also means to store something away, to keep it safe, even to hide it.

This is the way Jesus uses the verb *treasure* in the Sermon on the Mount, when he says, "Treasure up for yourselves treasure in heaven" (Matt 6:20). But Jesus does not say here how to lay up treasure in heaven, and he does not even say what that treasure you store in heaven might be. And, whatever it is, if it is stored away then it can't be available to you right now.

So when Jesus says, "Treasure up for yourselves treasure in heaven" (Matt 6:20), he leaves some important considerations up in the air.

But Jesus does tell us one thing that is vitally important to our spiritual life. It is important to our psychological and social lives, too. He may not say all that clearly *how* to store up treasure in

---

(Eleonore Stump, *Wandering in Darkness: Narrative and the Problem of Suffering* [Oxford: Clarendon, 2010], 432–33). Compare Saint Bernard, "By the very law of man's desire, which makes him want what he lacks in place of what he has and grow weary of what he has in preference to what he lacks, once he has obtained and despised all in heaven and on earth, he will hasten toward the only one who is missing, the God of all. . . . [W]hoever desires the greatest good can succeed in reaching it if he can first gain possession of all he desires short of that good itself" (Dil 19; CF 13:112); and Gregory the Great: "In this life, 'man is born to labor' [see Job 5:8], for every carnal person, in seeking to obtain [*appetit*] transitory things, is overcharging himself with the burden of his desires [*desiderium suorum se pondere affligit*]. . . . It is sore labor, with infinite pains to lay hold of that, which he that shall lay hold, knows can never remain for long" (Mor in Job 6.XIII.16).

heaven, nor *what* that treasure might be, nor what good it is to us when it is stored up. But he does tell us *why* to store up treasure in heaven. Why? "Because where your treasure is there your heart will be" (Matt 6:21).

As Jesus sees it, we can treasure up for ourselves treasures on earth, and we can treasure up for ourselves treasures in heaven. His point is that wherever we treasure them up, it is there that our heart will be.

Our heart is our consciousness, our love, our desire, our preoccupation, our attention; our heart is us. What we treasure and where we store it, there will we be, too. So our treasure and our treasuring up serve as mirrors to reveal to us our deepest consciousness, just as dreams and body language tell us infallibly what we really desire and what we really love and what we really fear.

We can easily make use of this mirror to check ourselves. Where is our heart? What do we think about? As monks, what do we turn to when we have a spare quarter of an hour? What do we do on a Sunday afternoon? What role does the Internet play in our life, or the smart phone? Where your treasure is, there your heart will be. Where is your heart? Where are you?

Later on in the gospel of Matthew Jesus tells someone *how* to store up treasure in heaven. It is when he tells the rich young man, "Go, sell what you have and give to the poor, and you will have treasure in heaven" (Matt 19:21). Does that word apply to everyone? Is Jesus saying that getting rid of all your possessions here on earth is the *way* to store up treasure in heaven?

For this particular person, at least, it is the method of treasuring up. It is the method of self-dispossession. And because Matthew took the trouble to record this word of Jesus, and because it has been repeated ever since in the liturgical assembly, we are not wrong to conclude that it is a method recommended to everyone who follows Jesus.

Saint Paul confesses that he made good use of this method: "For his sake I have suffered the loss of all things." At the same time, Paul makes clear what Jesus didn't; he tells us *what* the treasure is, too: "in order that I may gain Christ" (Phil 3:8).

As Paul says in Colossians, "Set your minds on things that are above, not on things that are on earth," for in Christ "are hid all the treasures of wisdom and knowledge" (Col 2:3; 3:2).

We have a homily of Saint Bernard's for the feast of Saint Martin of Tours. People used to say that Saint Martin was always "looking up at the sky as though he were out of his mind." Bernard comments, "Indeed, the man of God . . . was always looking up to heaven! For he knew . . . that his treasure was there, he knew that his Christ sat there at the right hand of God, he knew that he would never attain to what he desired until he reached that place. . . . His conversation was in heaven and his eyes were in his head" (Mart 14; see CF 54:225).

But then there is a sudden and unexpected shift in this biblical theme of treasure in heaven. After affirming that in Christ are hid all the treasures of wisdom and knowledge, Paul claims, "You have died and *your life is hid with* Christ in God" (Col 3:3). Now, it seems, in Christ *we ourselves* become the treasure hidden and laid up in heaven. Our very own life, our soul, in Christ, is our treasure even here on earth. "You joyfully accepted the plundering of your property," says the Letter to the Hebrews, "since you knew that you yourselves had a better possession and an abiding one," the preservation of your souls (Heb 10:34, 39). Saint Peter talks about "an inheritance which is imperishable, undefiled, and unfading, kept in heaven for you who by God's power are guarded through faith [more precious than gold] for a salvation ready to be revealed in the last time. . . . As the outcome of your faith you obtain *the salvation of your souls*" (1 Pet 1:4, 5, 9).

But then there is another shift, and things get totally turned upside down, as is only to be expected from a God who emptied himself, taking the form of a slave. "Surely," says Saint Bernard, "man is made as an emptiness, man is brought to nothing, man is nothing." And yet, Bernard observes, doesn't Job say, speaking to God, "What is man . . . that *you* set *your heart* upon *him?*" (Job 7:17; emphasis mine).

So, concludes Bernard, "How is one 'nothing' upon whom God has set his heart? Let us breathe a bit, my brothers, and if we are nothing in our own hearts, perhaps in the heart of God something different about us lies hidden."

"Father of mercies, Father of the miserable, *why* do you set your heart upon [*us*]," Bernard asks God, and then gives the answer: "I know, I know: *Where your treasure is, there your heart is also.* How then can we be 'nothing' if *we* are *your* treasure?" (Ded 5.3, 4; see CF 54:203; emphasis mine).

23

On Matthew 6:22-23

(Luke 11:34-36)

In the Sermon on the Mount Jesus says, "The eye is the lamp of the body" (Matt 6:22). Earlier in the Sermon he said, "Let your light so shine before men that they may see your good works" (Matt 5:16). In both of these sayings in the Sermon on the Mount Jesus makes a connection between inner light and outward actions.

"The eye is the lamp of the body." If your eye is a lamp, then if you close your eye it is like putting a lamp under a bushel basket. If you close your eye then your light cannot shine before others. In biblical terms, if your faith isn't expressed in righteous deeds, your faith is useless.

Just as for other people of his time, for Jesus the eye was an emitter of light, not just a receptor of light, as we understand the eye today. The eye, like the sun, contained its own light. Or better, as Jesus will go on to say, it was through the eye that the light in the body shone outward. The eye functioned by extramission, if that is a word, not just by intromission, by emitting light as a lamp does, not by taking it in, as a camera lens does.

So you find in the book of Sirach the contrast of human eyes with the eyes of the Lord, which are "ten times brighter than the sun" (Sir 23:19). As Proverbs says, "The light of the eyes gives joy to the heart" (Prov 15:30). When Saul's son Jonathan tasted honey, "his eyes brightened" (1 Sam 14:27). The eyes emit light: that is what people of Jesus' time understood, and the light the eyes emitted was inside the body. "His eyes," says John the Seer in the Book of Revelation, "were like a fiery flame" (Rev 1:14).

Jesus is saying that the disciple who is full of light lights up the world around him or her. The body would then be like a house in the evening where people were sitting down to Thanksgiving dinner. If the curtains on the windows were drawn back, people outside would see the light coming from the candles on the table within the house. The body is like that house with the candles burning inside, and the eyes are like those windows that let the inner light be seen by people passing by outside.

So Jesus goes on to say, "If your eye is healthy"—that is, if it is emitting light—then that shows that "your whole body is full of light" (Matt 6:22), just like a house on Thanksgiving Day.

This understanding of the eye is foreign to us because we know the physiology of the eye. We know that the eye does not give out light but takes it in from the outside; if the eye seems to sparkle, it is because it reflects back light coming from the outside. Jesus and his audience had a different understanding.

In any case, Jesus was using this image of the eye as a lantern and the body as being full of light as a parable or a metaphor. The point of the parable is in the paradoxical concluding exclamation: "If then the light in you is darkness, how great is the darkness?" (Matt 6:23b).

So what is the point?

As almost always, Jesus leaves it up to us to answer that question. We answer it by asking ourselves, in the terms of the parable, "Am I filled with light or with darkness? Is my eye good or is it bad?" If my eye is good and emitting light, then, yes, there is light in me. But if my eye is not emitting light, then it is bad, and that is a sure sign that "the light in" me "is darkness." In his commentary on Saint Matthew's gospel, Saint Chromatius of Aquileia (d. 406) warns Jesus' disciples against "veiling over and obscuring by infidelity the light people so desperately need."[1]

But what is this light, or, if that is the case, this light that is darkness? In answering that question we cannot go wrong by remembering what Matthew said earlier in his gospel. He quoted the prophet Isaiah: "*Land of Zebulun, land of Naphtali, toward the sea, across the Jordan, Galilee of the Nations—the people sitting in darkness saw a great light, and on those sitting in the region and the shadow of death, a light has risen upon them*" (Isa 8:23–9:1; 58:10; Ps 107:10; Matt 4:16 [#2, #3]).

For Matthew, Jesus coming to Capernaum from Nazareth is a light, a rising sun. As we said earlier (#3), Jesus does not come from outside the land of Zebulun and Naphtali, but from deep within it. Matthew is saying in his own way what John will later say in his, that Jesus is the Word made flesh, the light that shines in the darkness, a "bridegroom coming from his tent" to "his own home" (see John 1:14, 5, 11; Ps 19:6). Jesus of Nazareth comes to Capernaum, makes his home there, and then, at that time, starts the *kerygma*, the proclamation of the Gospel. His first words are the first rays of the rising sun: "Repent, for the kingdom of heaven is at hand."

So for Jesus, when he talks about the light that fills your whole body, he is talking about himself and his Gospel, which fills your whole life because you have received and welcomed him in repentance.

But, says the gospel of John, there is also this possibility: "people loved darkness rather than light" (John 3:19). So the light that has come into the world can also be darkness when, like seed falling on rocky ground, it is not received by the good soil of a pure

---

1. Chromatius of Aquileia, Tractate 5.1.3-4; second reading of the Office of Readings for the Memorial of Saint Barnabas, *The Liturgy of the Hours* III (New York: Catholic Book Publishing, 1975), 1464.

heart (see Matt 13:1-9; 5:8). There seems to be no gray area here. And so the eye that like a lamp lets the light out, or not, is either sound or bad.

We can understand what Jesus meant by a sound eye by looking at what he meant by a bad eye. Remember the parable later in Matthew about the workers in the vineyard (Matt 20:1-16). The ones hired last worked only an hour but were paid the same as the ones hired first, who had worked all day. When the latter complained about the disparity of wages, the householder said, "Am I not allowed to do what I choose with what belongs to me? Or do you begrudge my generosity?" (Matt 20:15). Literally he says, "Or is your eye bad because I am good?"

The bad eye is all that is hostile to generosity. The bad eye is jealousy of another person's good fortune and resentment at another person's goodness; it is selfishness and covetousness. "If one of your kindred is in need," says Moses in Deuteronomy, "you shall freely open your hand and generously lend what suffices to meet that need. Be careful not to . . . have a bad eye toward your brother who is in need and give him nothing. . . . When you give, give generously and not with a stingy heart" (Deut 15:7-10).

"Let your light so shine before men that they may see" (Matt 5:16). The light is the Gospel that fills our body, our life. Here Jesus is telling us that the Gospel is fundamentally magnanimity, munificence, and generosity, like scattered seed falling wherever, like sun and rain falling on good and bad alike (Matt 13:3-9; 5:45). Jesus' teaching about the inner light and the good and simple eye from which it shines out is about the coherence for Christians between inner states and outer acts.

"Out of the abundance of the heart the mouth speaks. The good person out of the good treasure brings forth good," though there is always the danger that the light within us be darkness, the danger of appearing beautiful outwardly while being inwardly filled with the bones of the dead (Matt 12:34-35; 23:27).

Saint Benedict tells us in the Prologue to his Rule, "The Lord waits for us daily to translate his holy teaching into action. . . .

We must, then, prepare our hearts and bodies for the battle of holy obedience to his instructions. . . . [So] while there is still time, while we are still in this body and have time to accomplish all these things by the light of life, we must run and do now what will profit us forever" (RB Prol. 35, 40-44).

24

On Matthew 6:25

(Luke 12:32)

Gregory the Great tells the story of Saint Benedict and the monastery's oil barrel. This was cooking oil, a staple of the Mediterranean diet.[1]

It was during a great famine in Campania, and the oil barrel was empty. Benedict had given almost everything away to the needy of the area. All that was left was a little oil in a glass jar when someone came to the monastery, asking, of course, for a little oil. Benedict told the cellarer, the monk in charge of the material goods of the monastery, to give the man that last little bit of oil in the glass jar.

When Benedict discovered later that the cellarer had not given the oil—for to have done so would have been contrary to the whole value system of a cellarer, who is to care for the goods of the monastery and especially to provide for the material needs of the monks[2]—why, Benedict became so furious that he commanded the little jar be thrown out the window to crash and break on the stones below—"so that nothing of the fruits of disobedience might remain in the monastery."

1. Gregory the Great, Dial 2.28.
2. See RB 31.

They did throw it out the window and it landed on the ground; but the jar did not break, nor was the oil in it lost. Benedict then said to give the oil to the man, and that is what they did.

"You," Jesus says in the Sermon on the Mount, "do not be anxious in soul or in body about what you are to eat or what you are to wear" (Matt 6:25). Soul and body are the entire person and his life, and food and clothes, are his interior and exterior, so Jesus' word really means, "Don't be anxious at all about anything of this mortal life of yours."

This is one of those sayings of Jesus that are called hard sayings. The cellarer of the monastery is paid, so to speak, *to* be anxious in the sense of taking great care for the physical well-being of the brothers, the prudent use of capital, and the maintenance of material goods.[3] Gregory says of Saint Benedict that he "had resolved to give all upon earth that he might have all in heaven,"[4] but certainly Benedict can't impose his own resolve and spiritual convictions on others, can he? Can Jesus impose his on us?

Don't be anxious.

Is this a command, a counsel, a wisdom saying, or what? Is "Do not be anxious" the same kind of speech as "Do not steal"?

Or is "Do not be anxious" more like Mark 9:25: "I charge you, come out of him, and enter no more into him"; that is, is this word of Jesus an exorcism?

Because anxiety can be like a demon. You can ask about your own experience of anxiety: *are* you anxious as a defining characteristic in the same way that you *are* a certain height or of a certain temperament, or is it rather that anxiety, as something from the outside, has taken *possession* of your interior?

In fact, anxiety is more often a state than a choice, a feeling than a thought; anxiety is a pressure that we are somehow powerless to push back against with good results. Anxiety is something undergone and endured. It is no small matter.

3. See RB 31.
4. Gregory the Great, Dial 2.28.

So maybe Jesus' word "Do not be anxious" *is* more like an exorcism than like a piece of self-help advice.

In Luke's version of this teaching of Jesus, Jesus goes on to say, "Do not be afraid any longer, little flock" (Luke 12:32). Anxiety is related to fear. Maybe fear is the root of anxiety, and the root of fear is uncertainty and the sense that there is nothing to stand on where there should be something firm. You fear, you are gripped by a deep uneasiness, and as the vise of uneasiness tightens you become anxious. You perceive that things precious and dear to you, things you treasure, are threatened from forces outside your control.[5]

These things can be values and customs that we have defined ourselves by, so when we think that these things are being threatened it feels that we ourselves are in mortal danger. Take what intruded itself worldwide in March of 2020, for example. It is even worse when the apparent source of those forces is the very thing or person you would hope you could trust to protect you and the things dear to you, but now realize that that thing or person is not trustworthy at all—a parent, a pastor, a pope, an abbot, a spouse.

Many children have every reason not to trust their parents. That lack of filial trust is tragic; it influences their whole lives and explains a lot of their relational problems, their chronic anxiety.

But the uneasy person distrusts himself first of all. And of course that distrust of yourself almost always gets translated into distrust of others and into the belief that others do not trust you. There must be a name for this psychological trick that attributes to and blames others for the feelings that plague us. You consider yourself unworthy of being loved; how can you not suspect anyone who shows you signs of friendship and affection? "Therefore, I tell you, do not be anxious." It is a hard saying.

"But seek first the kingdom of God and his righteousness, and all these things will be given you besides" (Matt 6:33), given you, that is, by God, your heavenly Father, who knows.

5. On anxiety and uneasiness, see Gabriel Marcel, *Problematic Man* (New York: Herder, 1967).

For Jesus, your heavenly Father who knows is the one thing, the only thing, that is reliable and trustworthy, but to trust that fact is itself not all that easy. It takes practice and more than being small-of-faith (see #35). The way to that trust is asceticism in the area of thought control and the kinds of expectations we set up.

On the other hand, Jesus' word of exorcism, "Do not be anxious," will drive out only the demon of the sick anxiety that stands in the way of and conceals a *necessary and holy anxiety* that is part of our relationship as unrighteous creatures with a fully righteous God. Jesus' exorcism does nothing to remove the *natural* uneasiness that follows from the fact of being free creatures of a transcendent God who are destined for transformation in that God.

I mean the salutary anxiety and unease that we are not as we should be—perfect, as your heavenly Father is perfect. It is a holy unease that is the opposite of complacency and is the door to all spiritual progress. This holy unease that is part of our sheer mortality in relationship to God is paradoxically free from fear and mistrust because imbued with faith, hope, and love. "O you of little faith" (Matt 6:30).

Gabriel Marcel writes, "Positive uneasiness . . . is the disposition which allows us to detach ourselves from the vise in which daily life squeezes us, with its hundreds of cares which end up by masking the true realities. *This* uneasiness is a principle of self-transcendence, it is a path which we have to ascend in order to attain to true peace,"[6] that is, to the kingdom of God and his righteousness and all these things given you besides (see Matt 6:33).

Saint Gregory concludes his story: when the brothers saw the little jar intact they all fell down in prayer. The lid on the empty oil barrel began to be heaved up by the oil increasing under it, which ran over the brim of the barrel upon the floor in great abundance.

---

6. Marcel, *Problematic Man*. I am unable to locate this quotation.

25

On Matthew 6:34

(see Luke 12:25; John 14:1)

Being a child stamps the whole life of Jesus' disciples. Being a child of the Father brings with it certainty, security, and courage. Let's look at each of these.

First, being a child brings certainty. It brings the certainty that we have a share in the kingdom of God:

> *The kingdom of heaven belongs to such as these,*
> *and it is not the will of my father in heaven*
> *that one of these little ones should perish.* (Matt 19:14; 18:14)

Second, being a child of God also brings with it an everyday security:

> *The Father knows what his children need;*
> *do not be anxious about the morrow.* (see Matt 6:32, 34; 7:11;
> Luke 12:30)

The daily bread we ask for day after day ends up, in fact, on our plate and in our stomach, not to mention the superessential bread that we are fed with from the altar (see #18).

And even if the daily bread is not forthcoming, and we know that it is not for too many of our brothers and sisters, the child is confident that his Father knows why, or if he does not know why, then he mourns over us and alongside us in our suffering.

Third, then, childhood gives us the courage to suffer. The certainty and the security of the child are in function of this courage to suffer. Life has its contradictions. Sometimes, it seems, life, and especially monastic life, is absolutely designed to end in failure.

In any case, categories like success and failure, useless and profitable, make sense only when measured against our desires, our intentions, and our aims.

If our aim is to seek first the kingdom of God and his righteousness, then we are in the world of the foolishness of God and the weakness of God, and that is the world of childhood (see Matt 6:33; 1 Cor 1:25).

In that world, who can be sure whether failure is not really success, if the cross is not really Glory? Only he who will be taken by surprise to hear when all is said and done, "Well done, good and faithful servant; you have been faithful over a little . . . enter into the joy of your Lord" (Matt 25:21).

The Letter to the Hebrews refers to the world of the folly of God when it says, "Let us go to [Jesus] outside the camp and bear the abuse he endured" (Heb 13:31).

Jesus lived in that world continually. The world of the folly of God outside the camp was the context of his ministry, teaching, and prayer. "At that time," Matthew says, "Jesus declared."

It was a time when it might have seemed to Jesus that his work had proved a failure; only the disreputable, the ragtag, the riffraff were following him. It was precisely at that time that Jesus declared, "I thank you, Father, . . . that you have hidden these things from the wise and the prudent, and revealed them to babes" (Matt 11:25).

In Dostoevsky's *Brothers Karamazov* a young lad asks Alyosha, "Tell me, Karamazov, am I very ridiculous now?" Alyosha responds, "Don't think about it. . . . What does it matter how many times a man is or seems to be ridiculous? Besides, nowadays almost all capable people are terribly afraid of being ridiculous, and are miserable because of it. . . . [E]ven children . . . are already beginning to suffer from [their fear of appearing ridiculous]. It's almost a madness."[1]

After the first visit of the rebels on Christmas Eve, 1993, Brother Christophe Lebreton of Atlas[2] wrote,

> Christmas.
> A dark night. The morning Star lights up each face. We
>   are all alive.
> And the light shines in the darkness, and the darkness
>   does not overcome it.
> It is enough to stand firm in the power of becoming
>   children of God,
> born here of God.[3]

A year later, Christophe wrote, "In the face of death, tell me that my faith—which is Love—will hold strong. Suddenly, I am terrified to believe."[4]

Courage in full bloom, like love and like faith, does not look like courage at all, like prayer, which is not perfect prayer if one knows he is praying.[5] Father Bruno Lemarchand had written, "Here I am before you, my God. . . . Here I am, rich in misery

---

1. Fyodor Dostoevsky, *The Brothers Karamazov, A Novel in Four Parts with Epilogue,* trans. Richard Pevear and Larissa Volokhonsky (New York: Farrar, Straus and Giroux, 2002), 557–58.

2. Christophe, with Bruno and Christian, were Trappist Cistercian monks of the monastery of Atlas, Algeria. With four of their confreres they were in 1996 apprehended and killed by political extremists. Rather than leave Algeria and return to their native France as the Algerian government urged them to do, they had remained with their Muslim neighbors in the solidarity of uncertainty and fear. The seven Martyrs of Atlas were beatified with twelve others in Oran, Algeria, in 2018.

3. In Bernardo Olivera, *How Far To Follow? The Martyrs of Atlas* (Petersham, MA: Saint Bede's, 1997), 61.

4. Olivera, *How Far,* 100.

5. See John Cassian, *Conference* 9.31: Abba Anthony used to say, "That is not a perfect prayer wherein a monk understands himself and the words which he prays" (Nicene and Post-Nicene Fathers, 2nd series, vol. 11, ed. Philip Schaff and Henry Wace [Buffalo, NY: Christian Literature Publishing Co., 1894], 1005).

and poverty, full of unspeakable cowardice. Here I am before You who are nothing but Mercy and Love. Before you, but solely by your grace, I am here whole and entire, with all my soul, all my heart, all my will."[6]

In Lent of 1996, just days before the abduction, Dom Christian de Chergé reflected in his journal, "through that experience [of Christmas Eve, 1993] we felt invited to be born again. The life of a man goes from birth to birth. . . . In our life there is always a child to be born: the son of God who each of us is."[7]

In the state of Gospel childhood, suffering is not just inevitable; it is a vocation, a call: those who belong to the kingdom can expect to be persecuted for it; those who belong to Jesus will be reviled for the sake of his name.

A death sentence is on our heads, living in "the second world" (see #21).

It was to these that Jesus addressed the Beatitudes: "Blessed are you, Happy are you." When Jesus connects blessedness with suffering, he is not selling masochism.

The blessedness does not come from the poverty, from the persecution; it comes solely from membership in the kingdom, which is the same as being a child of the Father; the blessedness of the kingdom is the certainty, security, and courage that constitute being a child.

This is surely the only way to read the fourth degree of humility in the Rule of Saint Benedict: "In truth, those who are patient amid hardships and unjust treatment are fulfilling the Lord's command: 'When struck on one cheek, they turn the other; when deprived of their coat, they offer their cloak also.' With the apostle Paul, they bear with false brothers, endure persecution, and bless those who curse them" (RB 7.42-43).

The problem of evil, of the Evil One, is left in the Father's hands. Nothing happens without God. Jesus believes that unconditionally.

6. Olivera, *How Far*, 100–101.
7. Olivera, *How Far*, 103.

Stronger than all questions, riddles, and anxieties is the one word, "Abba."

The Father knows.

The kingdom is for children. Children have certainty of their salvation in the world to come. Certain, they are secure and without anxiety in the present age.

Certain and secure, when they are squeezed and pressed by life and by the Evil One they are surprised to find themselves courageous.

On Christmas Day, 1995, Father Christophe made a Christmas creche. Contemplating the figures, he said, "Behold the lamb. He is here. Soon comes the marriage. [The Infant King]—stronger than murder—it is he, born in the midst of us, to be offered in our lives."[8]

We have not received a spirit of slavery, holding us in fear. With Christian, Christophe, and companions, we have received the spirit of children, the Spirit crying "Abba" (see Rom 8:15; Gal 4:6-7). And so we have the courage to pray.

8. Olivera, *How Far*, 119.

26

On Matthew 7:1-5

(Luke 6:37-42)

"Stop judging, that you may not be judged" (Matt 7:1). Jesus does not mean, "Don't use your critical ability to discern the time." He doesn't mean, "Don't choose between the narrow gate and the wide gate or between right and wrong." He doesn't mean, "Stop hearing the cause of the powerless in the face of those who abuse and take advantage of them." He doesn't mean, "Stop weighing options and making decisions."

Jesus has just said that you can't serve two masters (Matt 6:24). That means that you have to judge between them and take a stand in favor of one while forgetting about the other. We have to judge. "Stop judging, that you may not be judged" must refer to some other kind of judging.

At least we can be sure of this: that this other kind of judging was something almost everyone was doing: you don't take the trouble to say, "Stop it!" to what no one is doing.

Our translation gets it right: *Stop* judging, implying that up to this point you have the practice of judging, whatever we mean by judging.

When Jesus says stop judging he does not mean not to take evidence into account. He does mean the way you interpret the evidence; he means not taking all the evidence into account, especially evidence that could lead to a different conclusion. He means stop judging even without evidence, not generalizing something someone did or said once to mean that that person must be guilty of always saying or doing that thing. "Stop judging" means stop forming fixed and sealed conclusions about a person or a group of persons in such a way that you lock them up and then throw away the key.

What Jesus is prohibiting, I think, is the kind of judging that is condemning. Judging that is condemning is harsh, usually unfair, and biased; it is narrow, lacks sympathy, does not allow for repentance, and fails to try to understand. Someone "looking at the outward appearance and judging according to the outward appearance is prepared to think a splinter a plank and a spark a blazing fire," says Saint Bernard (SC 29.4; see CF 7:106).

But Jesus did not say just, "Stop judging." He said, "Stop judging, that you may not be judged." This has the same ring to it as what we say in the Lord's Prayer: "Forgive us our trespasses as we forgive those who trespass against us." "That you may not be judged"—by whom? By God, whose judgment is final and definitive and true.

In adding that last part, "that you may not be judged," Jesus changes the quality of interpersonal and communal relationships from mere social courtesy for the sake of getting along to divine eschatological significance. It is the same with forgiveness, or refusing to forgive. The consequences are not negligible. Remember the parable of the unforgiving servant? "So will my heavenly Father do to you unless each of you forgives his brother or sisters from his heart" (Matt 18:35)—unless each of you stops judging your brother or sister in those unfair and narrow ways.

How does Jesus know this about how God works? Because, as he says in the gospel of John, the Father has given all judgment to the Son, and Jesus is the Son, who is also God (John 5:22).

We can understand "that you may not be judged" in this way, too: that you may not be judged or condemned by yourself. For when we are habitually judgmental and critical and unforgiving, we condemn ourselves to extreme unhappiness. We set limits on what can and cannot be, what can and cannot be expected from other people, and we don't let anything, even evidence to the contrary, remove or penetrate those hard canons of the story we live by. Then God does not have to judge us; we have done it to ourselves.

When Bernard said *splinter* and *plank* just now he was drawing from this part of the Sermon on the Mount. Jesus goes right on to say, "Why do you notice the splinter in your brother's eye, but do not perceive the wooden beam in your own eye?" (Matt 7:3). The point is clear, I think; that's the purpose of an image like that drawn from life. My mother used to use the one from her Irish background about the pot calling the kettle black. Both pots and kettles were equally black from the hearth fire fueled by peat.

Maybe Jesus heard the version about the splinter and the plank working with Saint Joseph and other men of his trade in Nazareth or in Sepphoris. But I think he heard it from his mother, Mary. Men wouldn't take the trouble to say that to one another, but women, especially wives and mothers, would say it to their husbands and sons.

Men have a tendency to project their own troubles and faults and foibles onto other men, and then to offer to help the other person instead of fixing themselves first. Women notice this trait of men and point it out to them. Mary certainly had occasion to say to both Joseph and Jesus that they were noticing the splinter in someone else's eye but ignoring the plank in their own, and she would have said it with endearing and good-natured irony and humor. There are many of Jesus' sayings that can be traced back to his mother, I believe.

You can take the splinter and plank as an example of what Jesus had just said about not judging, but it seems it is really about trying to help people. "How can you say to your brother, 'Let me remove that splinter from your eye,' while the wooden beam is in your eye?" (Matt 7:4). First get yourself in order; only then try to correct or to help someone else.

Maybe this is another reason that we shouldn't judge others. Saint Paul wrote to the Christians in Rome, "By the standard by which you judge another you condemn yourself, since you, the judge, do the very same things" (Rom 2:1). Paul then makes the same point Jesus did, that judging people like that has ultimate consequences: the principle of "on earth as in heaven": "Do you suppose, then, you who judge [others] and yet do [the same thing] yourself, that you will escape the judgment of God?" (Rom 2:3).

"A man's heart and thoughts are more prone to suspect evil than to believe good," Saint Bernard told his brothers, "especially when the obligation of silence does not permit you, whose conduct is in question, to defend yourself, nor him who suspects you to lay bare the wound from which he suffers, that it might be healed" (SC 29.4; CF 7:106).

Bernard then gives some advice. It is excellent advice, but also the kind of advice that helps you understand why Bernard saw the monastic life as a martyrdom. He says, "When an offence is committed against you, a thing hard to avoid at times in communities like ours, do not immediately rush . . . to retaliate . . . ; nor, under the guise of administering correction, should you dare to pierce with sharp and searing words one for whom Christ was pleased to be crucified; nor make grunting, resentful noises at him, . . . nor adopt a sneering air."

Then comes the hard part: "Let your passion die within, where it was born; a carrier of death, it must be allowed no exit or it will cause destruction; and then you can say with the prophet, 'I was troubled and I spoke not'" (SC 29.5; CF 7:107).

27

On Matthew 7:6

(John 17:6-19)

We looked at Jesus' exhortation, "Do not judge," in the Sermon on the Mount (#26). That word was the second of a series of exhortations that come in the Sermon at the end of chapter six and the beginning of chapter seven of the gospel of Matthew. The first exhortation was "Do not be anxious" (#24), and the second was "Do not judge."

After that comes the third exhortation in the form of a parable, a colorful one, and also a little violent: "Do not give the holy thing to dogs or throw your pearls in front of pigs, lest they trample them with their feet and turning on you tear you to pieces" (Matt 7:6).

Jesus is probably repeating a common proverb rather than making it up. The exhortation has a poetic structure and actually forms a little chiasm, two pairs of phrases that form a mirror image of one another.

It is hard to know how his Galilean audience would have understood this parable. They would have been familiar with dogs, but not as pets that you would give food to. In the ancient world dogs were semi-feral scavengers and at times even served as food themselves, although wealthy people could probably afford to keep dogs as pets.

It is unlikely that pearls would have meant much to Jesus' Galilean audience except as an extravagant dream. Galilee was inland from the saltwater sea where pearl oysters lived. Maybe some fresh-water mussels in the Sea of Galilee would have produced the occasional pearl or provided mother of pearl for jewelry and so forth. But few Galileans would have had much contact with pearls, and probably no one would have had enough pearls that the idea of casting "your" pearls before swine would have made any sense.

(Having here planted the notion of pearls, later Jesus can tell a parable saying that the case of a merchant seeking fine pearls is like the kingdom of Heaven. The extravagant dream of finding an off-the-charts gorgeous pearl having come true for him, the merchant willingly reduces himself to the likes of Galilean farmers and fisher-folk, to the likes of a disciple of Jesus, to own it [Matt 13:45]. His purchase of it is peremptory of everything else.)

Pigs would not have been common, either, since they were unclean animals and forbidden to Jews. Remember the herd of pigs that Jesus told the Legion of demons to go into? They were on the other side of the Sea, the Gentile side (Matt 8:28–9:1; #36). As for "the holy thing," what is that? You can think of meat on sale at the butcher's after being sacrificed to idols (see 1 Cor 10:19), but that was a pagan practice, and there would not have been much of that in Galilee. For Jews, sacrifices took place only in the Temple in Jerusalem.

So this exhortation of Jesus about a holy thing, pearls, dogs, and swine wouldn't, I think, have really resonated with Jesus' Galilean audience.

Still, the way he worded it is pretty vivid; you can get the sense of it: take care of what is precious to you; take care whom you entrust it to or share it with. Not everyone respects and values the things you do, whether your faith and religious convictions—the holy thing—or your material possessions and personal interests—pearls. They will not only treat those things badly, but they will treat you badly, too. It is not enough for extremist groups to burn churches; they also kill priests and rape women and kidnap children.

When I finished my biblical studies in Rome back in 1992, I took a trip to the Holy Land with a friend. One day we went to

Jericho. We had just bought some fresh fruit for ourselves, including some big beautiful black plums. Walking along we came across a group of boys around twelve or thirteen. My friend, call him Nick, offered them our plums. I would never have done that but Nick was really generous and looked for ways to make contact with people. Nick's eye was good (#23). For some reason I knew what the boys would do; I could see it in their eyes. They took the plums and threw them at us. It was not really threatening or violent or anything; it was more a prank, but it said something.

Mostly, to me it said we lost our beautiful plums, our black pearls. They were precious to me, and, applying the images from the parable, Nick had given them to pigs, and the pigs trampled them, and the dogs turned on us.

What can we understand by "the holy thing" that Jesus exhorts us not to give to dogs? What are the precious pearls that we need to take care not to throw before pigs? What is the treasure? For whatever it is, where it is, there our hearts will be also.

Jesus had just a few minutes before taught us to pray, "Father, hallowed be thy Name" (Matt 6:9; #17), so for us, the Name of God is the holy thing. To give the name of God to dogs would be breaking the second commandment, not to take the Lord's name in vain. The Lord's name in the Lord's Prayer is entrusted to catechumens only at the end of their formation when they are judged ready to respect and hallow the name of God.

The precious or holy thing given to catechumens is the Lord's Prayer and the symbol of faith (the Creed). They understand that those gifts are not to be treated lightly. Saint Benedict says that aspirants to the monastery should not be given an easy entrance (RB 58.1). Similarly the late first-century Christian text called the *Didache* warns, "But let no one eat or drink of your Thanksgiving [literally, *eucharist*] but those who have been baptized into the name of the Lord, for concerning this also the Lord has said, Give not that which is holy to the dogs" (Did 9.5).

I think Catholics have to be careful, though, not to call dogs non-Catholic Christians who present themselves for Communion at Catholic Masses, or for that matter divorced and remarried Catholics who do the same. Besides, you can't imagine them trampling the Eucharist under their feet, or turning on you and tearing you to pieces, either.

"The temple of God is holy, and you are that temple" (1 Cor 3:17). So here is another holy thing not to throw to the dogs. Rather, "Present your bodies as a living sacrifice, holy and acceptable to God, your spiritual worship" (Rom 12:1). We can question ourselves on the care of our bodies: do we throw our bodies to the pigs of overeating and self-indulgence?

As monks, our very monastic consecration is a holy thing and a pearl of great price. Then even the least significant thing in the monastery is sacred, too, as Benedict says (RB 31.10). That would include intangible things like our use of time, our practice of *lectio*, our prayer, and our willingness to engage with one another in tender and nonjudgmental ways. Do we throw away our *lectio* and prayer time to YouTube, to email, to unhelpful reading? You know, these things have a way of turning on you, of tearing you to pieces however slowly.

Dioceses are selling sacred church properties for luxury development, and then there's the unspeakable fact of over fifty-five million abortions in the United States since 1973. These children are holy things. The angel Gabriel said to Mary at the Annunciation, "The Holy Thing begotten will be called Son of God" (Luke 1:35).

But you know, we are so self-centered. We always interpret Scripture as having to do with us, and usually as making some moral demand: do this, don't do that. What if when Jesus gave this exhortation, "Do not give the holy thing to dogs or throw your pearls in front of pigs," he was not addressing the audience but praying to his Father?

In fact, this exhortation is very much like the petition in the Lord's Prayer: "Lead us not into temptation, but deliver us from evil."

What if Jesus is giving his own version of the Psalm: *Father, do not give the soul of your dove to the beasts nor forget the life of your poor ones forever, but rather, turn your steps to these places that are utterly ruined, which the enemy has laid waste* like pigs trampling and dogs ripping (see Ps 74:19, 3)?

You might object that Jesus' exhortation is in the second-person plural but God is one. A thoughtful objection, but easily set aside. Didn't God himself say, "Let *us* make man in *our* image" (Gen 1:26)?

In this view, it is we, whom God made a little less than angels and crowned with glory and honor (Ps 8:6), who are God's own holy thing and pearls; we are, as Jesus said, the Father's gift to him (John 17:22) and precious in his eyes (see #22).

Maybe, then, Jesus is putting the burden on his Father not to abandon us in our sin, not to desert us in our backsliding and failures, not to lose patience with our adolescent efforts to save ourselves. We can make this prayer our own: "Father in heaven, do not give your holy thing to dogs or throw your pearls in front of pigs." It is a good prayer.

28

On Matthew 7:7-14

(Mark 11:24; Luke 11:9-13; 13:24)

"Your heavenly Father will give good things to those who ask him" (Matt 7:11b). Jesus says this in the Sermon on the Mount. We might wonder what the "good things" are that the heavenly Father gives for the asking.

We would not be wrong to go back to the Lord's Prayer: "This is how you are to pray" (Matt 6:9). In the Lord's Prayer we ask for six or seven things (see #16 through #21). These are the Good Things the heavenly Father will give to those who ask him.

What we ask for with the Lord's Prayer are things on the order of the one thing necessary, all that is implied by the phrase "the kingdom of God." They are the really needful things, but those for which the desire has to be cultivated, which cultivation is the work of Christian conversion. They are things that Jesus wants us to get familiar with to the point of *wanting* them, of needing them in the sense of really desiring and longing for them (see #15).

They are the things we pray for with the Lord's Prayer: the kingdom of heaven, the sanctity of God's name, the doing of God's will, which Jesus only prayed for at the end, in the Garden of Gethsemany the night before his passion, our daily bread, which is not immediately satisfying or intelligible, and, most troubling of all, the willingness to forgive and to be delivered from the temptation to settle for the satisfaction derived from the meeting of our ephemeral needs.

Jesus prefaced the Lord's Prayer with the assurance, "Your Father knows what you need before you ask him" (Matt 6:8b). It is an assurance that he echoes a short while after the Lord's Prayer, "But seek first the kingdom of God and his righteousness, and all these things will be given you besides" (Matt 6:33), that is, not the good things, but the things the pagans seek, clothes and food and shelter and all those things that while necessary for creatures are destined like creatures to pass away (Matt 6:25-32a), the things not to worry over because your heavenly Father knows you need them (#24).

The items that Jesus *does* tell us to pray for in the Lord's Prayer, then—"*this* is how you pray"—are not things like food, shelter, and clothing, needs that he says our Father will provide in any case.

Rather, Jesus intends the petitions of the Lord's Prayer to provoke in us a conversion of values, a real *metanoia* regarding what is important, which amounts to having the mind of the Christ of the Beatitudes—the poor in spirit, the hungry for justice—and of the Desert of Temptation—man does not live by bread alone (Matt 5:1-12; 4:1-11).

Close to the end of the Sermon on the Mount, Jesus gives what amounts to another version of the Lord's Prayer, only in general terms: "Ask and it will be given to you," he says; "seek and you will find; knock and the door will be opened to you. For everyone who asks, receives; and the one who seeks, finds; and to the one who knocks, the door will be opened." And he concludes, "your heavenly Father gives good things to those who ask him" (Matt 7:7-11). These are things the disciples of Jesus ask for. They are things on the order of the Beatitudes and of the Lord's Prayer. They are things that pertain to the kingdom of God.

Ask, seek, and knock. Of Israel of old, the prophet Hosea had said they would seek the Lord but not find him (Hos 5:6). But he had also imagined a door of hope that in the Song of Songs the Beloved himself knocks at, wanting to be found (Hos 2:17; Song 5:2), and whom finding, the Lover would not let go (Song 3:4). Beggars *ask*, scavengers *seek*, and pilgrims *knock*: they are the poor in spirit who know their need for God (Matt 5:3; #7). Immediately having come down from the mountain, Jesus will find two of them approaching him; they will leave him with good things that only I-Desire and Coming-I-Will-Heal can deliver (#30, #31). Even the merchant seeking fine pearls, whom Jesus will say the kingdom of heaven is like, makes himself a scavenger with respect to the pearl of great price he finds, freely suffering the loss of everything if only he might have that good thing (Matt 13:45).

The Father's sun, finally, and his rain, benefiting good and bad alike, are natural symbols of another good thing that children of the kingdom pray for: "I say to you, love your enemies, and pray for those who persecute you" (Matt 5:44). "All things whatsoever that you would have people do for you, so you yourselves do for them" (Matt 7:12).

Jesus anticipates our shrinking back a bit from his tampering with our values and our comfort zones. He immediately comes in with a word of encouragement: "Enter through the narrow gate, for the gate is wide and the road broad that leads to destruction, and those who enter through it are many. How narrow the gate and constricted the road that leads to life, and those who find it are few" (Matt 7:13-14). In that word, by the way, is where you find the meaning of the name of our Order, the Strict Observance.

But then there is this story about Abba Moses of Scetis. Some fathers came to visit, and he used all the little water he had left to cook lentils for them. Moses got worried and went in and out of his cell until a cloud of rain came and filled all the cisterns around. The visitors asked him why he kept going in and out, and he said, "I was arguing with God, 'You brought me here, and now I have no water for your servants who came to me.' That is why I was going in and out; I was going on at God till he sent us some water."[1]

---

1. *The Sayings of the Desert Fathers, Alphabetical Collection,* trans. Benedicta Ward, CS 59 (Kalamazoo, MI: Cistercian Publications, 1975), Moses 13.

Have you ever seen the just man forsaken, or his children begging
  for bread?
The just perish, but no one takes it to heart.
Turn your eyes away from me. They disturb me.

29

On Matthew 7:24-27

After reproducing Jesus' Sermon on the Mount, Matthew says, "The crowds were amazed at his teaching, because he taught them as one who had authority and not as their scribes" (Matt 7:28-29).

There is an ambiguity about why the crowds were amazed. What was it about the Sermon on the Mount that left them amazed? Were they amazed by the content of Jesus' teaching, or by the manner of its delivery? Was the authority they recognized in the message, or was the authority in the person, the message's medium?

In our digital culture it is clear that the medium—the post, the tweet, the video, and so on—has the authority. The medium has become the message.

But for the crowds who heard Jesus it was the same. Jesus was the Word made Flesh. Jesus was at one and the same time the message—the Word—and the medium—Flesh.

Jesus concludes his Sermon with an exhortation: "Everyone then who hears these words of mine and does them will be like a wise person [*anēr*] who built his house upon the rock, and the rain fell, and the floods came, and the winds blew and beat upon that house, but it did not fall, because it had been founded on the rock" (Matt 7:24-25). Jesus is talking about his words—"these words of mine"—but he is also talking about himself, his very person in human and divine natures.

The foundation of rock that the church is built upon is the words of Jesus, but the words *are* Jesus, so that Paul can say "no other foundation can anyone lay than that which is laid, which is Jesus Christ" (1 Cor 3:11). In the liturgy we rightly give the same reverence to the book of the gospels that we do to the eucharistic species.

Later in the gospel of Matthew Jesus will echo this teaching about building on rock, but this time it will be Jesus himself who is the wise builder. He will build his church on the rock that is Peter (Matt 16:18). And if now Jesus envisions rain and river and wind assailing the house, then he will envision the gates of Hades trying to overpower the church.

The two passages, Matthew 7:24-25 and Matthew 16:18, are parallel. Jesus' words are the foundation, but Jesus himself in his divine personhood and two natures is the foundation, a status that in Matthew 16:18 becomes transferred by his own authority to Peter, the hierarchical nature of his church, which he himself builds. Jesus is the wise man whose home is the church, founded on his word as proclaimed and interpreted in history by the confessing and authoritative hierarchy of the church.

Paul, who affirmed that Christ himself is the foundation, will have no problem also affirming that the foundation of the structure, "a dwelling place of God in the Spirit," is the apostles and prophets (Eph 2:20, 22).

The gates of Hades will not overpower the church (Matt 16:18). What are the gates of Hades?

I think a good translation of the phrase is "hellish gates." The purpose of gates is to allow no one in and no one out. Gates are defenses. Hellish gates are reactions provoked by fear, fear of what might come in from an unknown world and fear of what will happen if we go out of our familiar world.

The hellish gates of fear and defensiveness are different from the gates of the New Jerusalem, the dwelling of God with humankind. There are twelve gates to that new city, but they are never shut, not even at night, because there will be no night (Rev

21:2, 3, 12, 25). When the hellish gates of fear do not prevail, the city is confidently open and free.

On the evening of the Resurrection the disciples were behind closed doors because of fear. These were the gates of hell prevailing. But the risen Lord passed right through and said, "Peace" (John 20:19). We erect the hellish gates of fear where there is no cause for fear. When the church has assimilated the words of the Word and the Word himself, then she can be open with the boldness of the martyrs, without fear.

In the Sermon on the Mount it is not hellish gates seeking to prevail over the church, but rain, river, and wind assailing the disciples. Rain, river, and wind are all forces of nature (Matt 7:24-27). But there is a difference among them worth noting: the rain is from heaven, the river from earth, and the wind—whence it comes and whither it goes we know not.

So maybe the rain, river, and wind as natural phenomena stand for the forces of history that in every generation and in every place threaten the disciples of Christ, who, as well-prepared catechumens, build their house on the foundation of Jesus' words.

But the great commission at the end of Matthew's gospel suggests something else. It was these very catechumens whom Jesus had in mind when he issued the great commission to his apostles: "Go, and make disciples of all nations, baptizing them in the name of the Father, the Son, and of the Holy Spirit, teaching them to observe all that I have commanded you" (Matt 28:19-20).

So the rain, river, and wind are Father, Son, and Holy Spirit, the Trinitarian God in whose name catechumens are baptized. If they have not been prepared, if they have not been brought to wisdom, if they have not grounded their faith on Jesus, the only foundation, and upon his word, then the force of the Trinitarian God in whose Name they will be baptized will be for their downfall and destruction.

The Trinitarian God is the force of love that is stronger than death and stronger than the hellish gates of fear (see Song 8:6).

It will be a reality and a truth too much for one founded only on the sand of ego to bear up under, and so that one will fall away.

> How long will you attack one man to break him down?
> *Have you considered my servant Job?*
> Your torrents and all your waves swept over him.
> *Many are the trials of the just, but the Lord delivers him from
>   them all.*
> Like chaff before the wind? I wait, in the muddy clay.

30

On Matthew 8:1-3

(Mark 1:40-44; Luke 5:12-14)

Jesus "taught as one having authority," and his authority evoked a response: amazement—"the crowds were astonished" (Matt 7:28-29). Saint Matthew tells us that after his account of the Sermon on the Mount.

Authority and amazement. You might say that the crowds recognized Jesus' authority in their response of amazement.

It is like love or desire. You encounter someone and find in response that you have fallen in love, and in that response you recognize that what you encountered is desirable.

The scribes of Jesus' time had authority that came from position, tradition, and expectation, but they did not evoke amazement. Jesus did, and in their response to Jesus the crowds recognized real authority. Recognizing, they followed him: "When Jesus came down from the mountain, great crowds followed him" (Matt 8:1).

"And then a leper approached [and] did him homage" (Matt 8:2).

In the Old Testament there are four stories about people who have leprosy. The first is in Numbers. Two of the stories are in the Second Book of Kings, and the last is in the Second Book of Chronicles.

In Numbers, Miriam, Moses' sister, is struck with leprosy.[1] It was the Lord who did it. It would take a long time to defend the Lord for striking Miriam with leprosy—which he says was like spitting in her face and she'd just have to put up with the shame—so I won't try (Num 12:9-15).

In Second Kings Naaman is the army commander of the king of Aram. Naaman was highly esteemed, respected, and valiant, "but . . . [he] had been struck with leprosy" (2 Kgs 5:1).

The other story in Second Kings is about four anonymous Israelites who had also been struck with leprosy (2 Kgs 7:3). You have to like these guys. They are companions in their misery. They sit by the city gate begging, but it is useless because famine has gripped the land, and anyway the city, Samaria, is under siege by the Arameans. They say, "Why should we sit here until we die? If we decide to go into the city, we shall die there, for there is famine in the city. If we remain here, we shall die too" (2 Kgs 7:3-4). So they decide to defect to the Arameans.

When they get to the Arameans' camp, though, they find it deserted. Because of a trick the Lord had played, all have fled the camp and left their belongings behind. So these four guys take advantage of the situation. They go into house after house and eat and drink and then carry off whatever they can of value and return for more.

After a spree of looting, though, they say, "We are not doing right. This is a day of good news, and we are keeping silent" (2 Kgs 7:8-9). So they go back and report what they discovered to the palace in Samaria.

Second Chronicles tells about Uzziah. He became king in Jerusalem at the age of sixteen and reigned for fifty-two years. Maybe it was too long a run, for after a while "he became arrogant to his own destruction" (2 Chr 26:16).

---

1. The Hebrew word is a participle of a verb with a passive sense, meaning "to be struck [with leprosy]." In two of the stories it is the Lord who is the implied active agent of the verb.

At one point Uzziah wants to take over the priests' job in the temple; when the priests stand up to him, Uzziah gets angry. He is holding the thurible at the time, because he wants to do the censing, so there is a nice connection between the hot thurible and Uzziah's anger. As a result of his outburst the Lord strikes him with leprosy.

Even so, and in spite of his arrogance and anger, Uzziah seems to have left a good memory: "He did what was right in the sight of the Lord" (2 Chr 26:1-4), a pretty good thing to say about a king. When Uzziah died, even though they said, "he had been struck with leprosy," they buried him with the other kings (2 Chr 26:23).

In these four cases of people with leprosy we note that the afflicted persons are not identified with their affliction. You could even say they were victims: they all had been *struck with leprosy.* The leprosy is one thing, the person another; the condition does not define the person.

On the contrary, at least in the case of Naaman and that of the four Israelites, the affliction helped create the occasion for the person's virtue to become evident. In Uzziah's case, even though the leprosy was a punishment for his acting out a defect of temperament and character, neither his acting out nor the punishment for it obliterated his deserved good reputation. In the case of Miriam, it was his own reputation that the Lord should have worried about. The people patiently waited till she was cured. She suffered no shame and served forever after as a reminder that leprosy could be cured (Deut 24:9).

For all these persons maybe their leprosy was like the "thorn in the flesh" and the scourge of Satan that Paul said he was afflicted with. It was the way for them to learn that God's "power is made perfect in weakness" (2 Cor 2:9).

Matthew 8:2 says that a leper approached Jesus. The leper goes unnamed. But later in the gospel of Matthew there is a leper whose name we are given. He is Simon of Bethany. Jesus visited his house just before the Last Supper and the passion, and it was in Simon's house that a woman approached Jesus and poured expensive perfume on Jesus' head (Matt 26:7). "Simon the leper" is how Matthew identifies this man (Matt 26:6).

It makes you ask, what leper?

In the gospel of Matthew there is only one leper Jesus has met before he goes to Simon's house. It is the one identified as a leper in Matthew 8:2, the one who "approached [Jesus and] did him homage" as soon as Jesus came down from the mountain after the Sermon on the Mount. It is reasonable to conclude, then, that when Matthew identifies Simon of Bethany as "the leper" it is this leper that he is referring to, the one whom Jesus touched with his hand and made clean (Matt 8:3).

Is Matthew identifying Simon with his disease when he calls him "Simon the leper"? Taking the same line as the Old Testament's presentation of people with this disease, maybe not. Rather, he is simply saying, "This Simon is the leper I told about that Jesus cured." Matthew would be identifying Simon not by Simon's former affliction but by the memorable gesture on the part of Jesus that took the affliction away.

Even so, it is possible that Simon still thought of himself as "Simon the leper" in the same way that someone sober for forty years identifies herself as Sarah the recovering alcoholic. She knows that on some level she must always identify with her illness, because if she forgot where she came from she would be presumptuous and ungrateful, and she would lose the sense of where she still needed to go.

If she forgot where she came from and how she had arrived where she was now, she would be likely to return to that painful place.

So if Simon forgot that he was once "the leper" and that Jesus' hand, his body summarized in five fingers, had touched and cleansed him, it would be a forgetting, the consequences of which were dreadful to think about. As it turned out, ever since then whenever this gospel has been proclaimed, what Jesus did for Simon the leper has also been told in memory of him (Matt 26:13).

And so with us. If we are grateful and amazed, let us recognize the source; then we will not be presumptuous but rather forbearing and patient with our brothers.

31

On Matthew 8:5-13

(Luke 7:1-10; John 4:43-54)

Last week we considered the four stories in the Old Testament about people who were said to be lepers (#30). We did that inspired by the leper who approached Jesus when Jesus had come down from the mountain where he had delivered the Sermon on the Mount. The leper was the first person he encountered, although it also says that many crowds followed Jesus (Matt 8:1-2).

We can imagine Jesus engaging with various people in the crowds, but because it says, "many crowds followed him," not "many crowds were with him," we can also imagine a solitary Jesus walking quite alone, the amazed crowds already keeping a respectful and awed distance from him.

In any case, this leper approached Jesus and paid him homage, or bowed before him, and spoke.

But these are things you do when you go to the temple or to a church: you approach, you kneel down or bow, and then you express your desire. The difference here is that this leper did not speak about *his* desire but about Jesus': "If you desire, you can cure me" (Matt 8:2). Is it a petition? Is it just a statement of fact? Is it a dare? Is it a test?

It is a very good prayer, whatever else it is. It is a prayer meant to awaken someone's good will to do what is beyond your ability to do for yourself but is in his power to do for you. And then it waits; it does not presume or demand.

In reply to the leper who said, "If you desire, you can make me clean," Jesus said, "I desire," and, while stretching out his hand and touching him, "be cleansed" (Matt 8:3). The reply has all the elements of a sacrament: a word, a gesture, a touch.

Now Matthew tells about a centurion in Capernaum who repeats what the leper did: he approaches Jesus and beseeches him (Matt 8:5).

But what he says—"Lord, my servant is lying paralyzed at home in terrible distress" (Matt 8:6)—is like what Mary said at the wedding in Cana: "They have no wine" (John 2:3). Both the centurion and Mary simply place a situation of need before Jesus. This is again a form of prayer. It is an implied petition.

In reply to the centurion who lays before Jesus the condition of his servant, Jesus says, "Coming, I will heal him" (Matt 8:7). This reply, like the one to the leper, "I desire," is an autobiographical statement. Both are self-definitions. Jesus *is* "I Desire," and he *is* "Coming I will heal." They are Jesus' exegesis of the incarnation; in other words, "I am loving Jesus."

In the last talk we identified Simon the leper, whom Jesus visits in Bethany just before his passion, with the leper whom Jesus cleansed in Matt 8:3 (#30). In the same way, when Matthew describes the crucifixion of Jesus and refers to "the centurion" who is a witness of the crucifixion (Matt 27:54), it is natural to ask, "What centurion?" and to conclude that it is the same centurion whose servant was paralyzed.

At the crucifixion the centurion makes what is certainly a profession of faith: "Truly, this was [a] son of God" (Matt 27:54). But it is also a conclusion, the result of a great deal of pondering and probably suffering ever since he had heard Jesus say of him, "Truly, not even in Israel have I found such faith" (Matt 8:10).

It was only at that word of Jesus, a word that issued from Jesus' own amazement, that the centurion knew he had faith at all— knew, and for the first time could name, that what had brought him to Jesus and had moved him to say, *Domine non sum dignus ut intres sub tectum meum; sed tantum dic verbo et sanabitur anima mea,* was faith (although the centurion did not say *anima mea,* my soul; he said, *puer meus,* my servant/boy).

How could that centurion have ever imagined that his words of profound respect and humility spoken out of great personal need, words that made Jesus marvel, would be repeated by great multitudes that no one could number, from every nation, tribe, people, and tongue, in every corner of the world from that moment on and forevermore (see Rev 5:9)?

"Lord, I am not worthy that you should enter under my roof, but only say the word, and my soul will be healed." When we say the centurion's words at Mass we are not as he was when he first approached Jesus about his servant. At Mass, we are responding directly to John the Baptist: *Ecce, Agnus Dei,* "Behold, the Lamb of God" (John 1:29), and in the Book of Revelation it is the Lamb who is "worthy": *Dignus est Agnus, qui occisus est,* "worthy is the Lamb that was slain" (Rev 5:12).

So at Mass, looking at the elevated Host just before receiving Communion, we speak the *words* the centurion used when he pleaded on behalf of his servant, but *as* he was at the cross. They are words of commitment and of faith: "Lamb of God, Crucified Son of God, I am not worthy; you alone are worthy. Say but the word and my soul shall be healed."

And then the word is spoken: "The Body of Christ," "the Blood of Christ," to which we say, "Amen," that is, "Truly, you are Son of God. I believe it."

The one who is I-Desire and Coming-I-will-heal has desired to come and to heal us. It is loving Jesus.

In an article I read once the author recalled that when she said these words of the centurion at Mass one Sunday, they struck her in a way that catapulted her right out of the church. "Lord, am I not worthy?" She had had enough of people telling her she was not worthy. She was especially tired of hearing that message from the church in countless subtle and sometimes overt ways.[1]

---

1. I read this article several years before this talk was written. I did not note its author or the book it was in.

So she left. She *was* worthy, she affirmed. You can understand that woman. I can.

Another article, by Michael Sean Winters, says that the centurion's words are "the most beautiful words in the world." Why? Sort of agreeing with the woman, he believes "in our time," to say "I am not worthy" is "quite counter-cultural, confronting the cult of self-esteem head-on. . . . We live in a Pelagian age in which we think we really do earn our way to heaven." We need to grasp that "it is in the Cross of Christ that we are justified before the Throne of Grace, and only there."

Mainly, though, it takes humility to say what the centurion did, and, Winter goes on, "the second one tries to focus on the cultivation of one's own humility, it melts like a snowflake in the palm of one's hand, melted by pride."[2]

"My soul shall be healed." What is a soul, an *anima*? Winters says that it is "something that unites the human race." Whatever *anima* is, in the centurion's prayer that we use at Mass it means that "in our deepest, darkest, most broken selves, the parts where we do not want to let the light shine, where we prefer not even to consider because it just hurts too much, Jesus can shine His light and bring healing."[3]

The story in Matthew about the centurion and his servant ends like the dismissal at Mass: "'Go; be it done for you as you have believed.' And the servant was healed at that very moment" (Matt 8:13).

So the point, finally, is not my soul but Jesus' power and word and touch. The point is the healing.

2. Michael Sean Winters, "The Most Beautiful Words in the World," https://www.ncronline.org/blogs/distinctly-catholic/most-beautiful-words-world, 2013.
3. Winters, "The Most Beautiful Words."

32

On Matthew 8:14-15

(Mark 1:29-31; Luke 4:38-39)

"And when Jesus had entered the house of Peter he saw his mother-in-law lying sick with a fever. And he touched her hand, and the fever left her, and she rose up and went on serving him" (Matt 8:14-15).

We have seen twice that just after the Sermon on the Mount in Matthew's gospel someone approaches Jesus. First it is a leper, and then it is a centurion with a paralyzed servant (#30, #31). But even before that we heard Jesus say, "the kingdom of heaven has drawn near" (Matt 4:17; #3). Everything that follows that announcement shows what he meant by it.

It is in Capernaum on the north shore of the Sea of Galilee. Jesus cleanses the leper with a touch of his hand and a word, and he cures the centurion's servant from a distance with just a word. Now he goes into Peter's house.

This was Simon Peter, the rock on which Jesus would build his church (Matt 16:18; see #29). When Matthew was writing his gospel the building of the church was already well underway.

Today in Capernaum there is a modern church building, circular and low, made of concrete and a lot of clear glass, built over the place where archeologists in the twentieth century have excavated what is believed to be this very house of Peter. As one article explains, "The house was simple, with coarse walls and a roof of earth and straw. Like most early Roman-period houses, it consisted of a few small rooms clustered around two open courtyards."[1]

Reporting the findings of the archeologists, the article says that "in the years immediately following Jesus' death . . . [this] house no longer functioned as a residence but instead had become a place for communal gatherings," and that excavators have uncovered "more than a hundred graffiti scratched into [its] walls. Most of the inscriptions say things like 'Lord Jesus Christ help thy servant' or 'Christ have mercy.' They are written in Greek, Syriac or Hebrew and are sometimes accompanied by etchings of small crosses or, in one case, a boat."

When Matthew writes "Peter's house," then, he is referring not just to the place that Peter once lived in, but also to the place that Christians had already appropriated, known, and used as a holy place and as a church.

More than that, for Matthew "Peter's house" was every place at any time where Christians gathered in the name of Jesus. That gathering was the house of Peter; it was the church built on the Rock of Peter, and even if it was only two or three, Jesus was in their midst (Matt 18:20). We here this morning are Peter's house.[2]

Jesus entered Peter's house and saw Peter's mother-in-law laid up with a fever. Matthew uses the same word, *laid up*, that was used for the centurion's paralyzed servant, so we are meant to see a connection between these two events (#31). Both passages, along with the cleansing of the leper (#30), tell us what it means that the kingdom of God has come near. That means it is not far. It can touch you and speak to your concerns when nothing else can, when you are "laid up," literally, when you have been thrown down (*beblēmenos*).

---

1. For archeologists on Peter's house see, for instance, https://www.biblical archaeology.org/daily/biblical-sites-places/biblical-archaeology-sites/the-house -of-peter-the-home-of-jesus-in-capernaum/.

2. On the day I gave this talk, my monastic community was gathered for a celebration in which six brothers received the Sacrament of the Anointing of the Sick.

In a single sentence four things happen in Peter's house—in the church: Jesus touched the woman's hand, the fever left her, she arose, and she went on ministering to him (Matt 8:15). This brief description has all the characteristics of a sacrament. The Catechism says that "Jesus' words and actions during his hidden life and public ministry were already salvific. . . . The mysteries of Christ's life are the foundations of what he would henceforth dispense in the sacraments," which "manifest and communicate to humans . . . the mystery of communion with the God who is love, One in three persons" and "bear fruit in those who receive them."[3]

In particular, the healing of Peter's mother-in-law is the sacrament of the Anointing of the Sick. As the Catechism says, "By the sacred anointing of the sick and the prayer of the priests the whole Church"—Peter's house—"commends those who are ill to the suffering and glorified Lord, that he may raise them up and save them. And indeed she exhorts them to contribute to the good of the People of God by freely uniting themselves to the Passion and Death of Christ."[4]

So Peter's mother-in-law arose and kept on serving him: Jesus, his Body, the Church. Continued to serve . . . the Body of Christ, in Peter's house. And so may it be for our six brothers.[5]

3. CCC 1115, 1118, 1131.

4. CCC 1499; Second Vatican Council, *Lumen Gentium*, 11.

5. The Greek verb for "served" is in the imperfect tense, suggesting a continuous action over an indefinite time.

33

On Matthew 8:16

(Mark 1:32-34; Luke 4:40-41)

"Evening having come, they brought to him many who were demon-possessed, and he cast out the spirits by a word and healed all who were sick" (Matt 8:16).

The scene is still at Peter's house in Capernaum where Jesus touched Peter's mother-in-law and the fever left her (Matt 8:14-15; #32).

Evening had come. When had the day started? Matthew does not say. Matthew draws our attention to the fact of its being evening by never having mentioned morning or daybreak in the astronomical sense. By saying that it was evening but without having said anything about morning or noon, Matthew intends to draw a connection between what Jesus does and the evening, the declining of day.

It is in the evening that Jesus expels spirits and heals all who were sick. The sun was going down on these tormented people. They were sitting in darkness and in the shadow of death (see Matt 4:16). It was the eleventh hour. It is always evening. This seems to be Matthew's message.

When we put it in those terms, then we recall that Matthew has talked about a new dawn. That was back in chapter four. It was when Jesus went to Capernaum from Nazareth right after his temptations in the desert. Matthew says that his going there was so that what was spoken by the prophet Isaiah might be fulfilled:

*Land of Zebulun, land of Naphtali, toward the sea, across the
Jordan, Galilee of the Nations—the people sitting in darkness
saw a great light, and to those sitting in the region and the
shadow of death, a light has dawned upon them.* (Isa 8:23–9:1;
58:10; Matt 4:16; #2)

So Jesus himself was the dawn and the daybreak for these tormented people, demon-possessed and others, whose whole life
had been a prolonged evening headed toward an eternal moonless
night.

We already saw the effects of the Messianic dawn in chapter
four when "they brought him all the sick, those afflicted with
various diseases and pains, demon-possessed, lunatics and paralytics, and he healed them" (Matt 4:24; #6).

These two comments by Matthew, one in chapter four and one
in chapter eight, about Jesus healing people, including demon-
possessed people, form a frame around the Sermon on the Mount
and the three particular cures that follow the Sermon: the leper, the
centurion's servant, and Peter's mother-in-law. The kingdom of God
is near; it is a new dawn, a daybreak casting its light through preaching and through sacramental action, word, and works of mercy.

It is a picture not just of Jesus but of the church he founded
upon the Rock of Peter. Just as in chapter four when Matthew
says that Jesus' ministry is to fulfill the prophet Isaiah, so he does
now in chapter eight: "This was to fulfill what was spoken by the
prophet Isaiah, 'He took our infirmities and bore our diseases'"
(Matt 8:17; Isa 53:4). Isaiah is talking about the Suffering Servant,
"a man of sorrows knowing pain," upon whom the Lord laid the
guilt of us all (Isa 53:3, 6).

Jesus, then, as Messiah and bringer of the kingdom, is not only
a new dawn; in the incarnation he totally immersed himself in, to
the point of identifying himself with, our evening, our night, our
death. Our guilt. There is a mystery here that is too deep for words,
that calls for our reverent contemplation of Jesus Christ, publicly
portrayed as crucified before our very eyes (see Gal 3:1).

I sometimes wonder about these people Jesus cured, especially the demon-possessed. We usually don't know what happened to them afterward. If we think of our own demon or our own drawn-out infirmity, whatever it is, there is a point where we have identified with it. Then, if it is suddenly taken away like the dawn scattering the darkest night, we don't know who we are anymore. Other people don't know us anymore, either. "Isn't this the one who used to sit and beg?" "No, he just looks like him" (John 9:8, 9). How do you adjust to the new you? When the excuse for your resentment has been taken away, how do you stop being resentful when being resentful is who you have become?

So there is a fear of the Messianic dawn, a fear of Jesus that is real and understandable. By his taking our guilt upon himself, our infirmities, we are left without moorings. We then transfer our resentment to Jesus. As José González Faus says, Jesus "incarnates the . . . Servant of the Lord . . . : he comes to serve and not to be served. And he serves by carrying on his shoulders all the miseries and pains of a suffering humanity, to the point of giving his life. . . . But it is only through that serving, which serves with the greatest of love, that God makes Jesus into the fount of new life for all."[1]

Precisely because he "took upon himself our suffering and our anguish" Jesus could go on to say, "Come to me, all who labor and are heavy laden, and I will give you rest" (Matt 11:28)—an invitation that is just another reason for fearing Jesus.

The Cistercian monk, the Order, each community, is mission territory. It always has been, always will be. This is our vocation. Louis Lekai, the Cistercian historian, said that the monks in Europe who emerged from the ruins of the twenty years of violence there at the end of the eighteenth century were no longer privileged creatures, reverenced and sure of themselves because they belonged to a great Order. Rather, they were just poor men in

---

1. See José González Faus, *Fear of Jesus: A Diagnosis*, CJ Booklets 136 (Barcelona: Cristianisme i justicia, 2009), 23.

search of God in the midst of a society that had very different goals.[2]

Somewhere I read that when he was abbot general of the Order, Bernardo Olivera quipped, "With the armor of the holy rule, the helmet of holy observance, and the sword of holy tradition, I still have a very hard time defending myself—from Jesus."

2. Louis J. Lekai, *The Cistercians: Ideals and Reality* (Kent, OH: Kent State University Press, 1977), 179–92.

34

On Matthew 8:18-22

(Luke 9:57-62)

"And one scribe came up and said to him, 'Teacher, I will follow you wherever you might go'" (Matt 8:19). So Saint Matthew continues his gospel. This is right after Jesus healed Peter's mother-in-law and cast out spirits with a word (#32, #33).

"And one scribe came up and said." The verse right before this one provides the context for the scribe's approach and for what he said to Jesus. Matthew writes, "Now seeing a crowd around him Jesus gave the order to go to the other side" (Matt 8:18). It is then that the scribe comes up and says, "Teacher, I will follow you wherever you might go." It is between Jesus' seeing the crowd and his actually getting into the boat and leaving that the one scribe approaches. The scribe interrupts Jesus' movement.

Jesus is in Capernaum. It's when he sees the crowd there that he gives orders regarding the boat, but it is only after the scribe's interruption that he gets in it and goes to the other side. The "other side," that is, the other side of the Sea of Galilee from Capernaum, is the country of the Gadarenes. Matthew tells us this just ten verses later (Matt 8:28).

It is a futile move though, because there, on the other side, after he casts the demons out of the two demoniacs, "the whole city goes out to meet him" (Matt 8:34; #36). So he goes from one crowd to another crowd.

Not only that: that second crowd "begged him to leave the area," with the result that Jesus immediately gets back into the boat and again goes across the Sea "to his own city" (Matt 9:1; #36). (You might think his own city was Nazareth, but it is Capernaum. In chapter four Matthew told us that Jesus left Nazareth and began to make his home in Capernaum [Matt 4:13; #1]). No sooner does he arrive back in Capernaum than "they brought him a paralytic" (Matt 9:2; #37).

It seems as though Jesus is looking for something like a monastic enclosure where he can be kept safe from people, but he's having no success. The safest place he has found is the boat, but even the boat seems to betray him.

"Now seeing a crowd around him Jesus gave the order to go to the other side. And one scribe comes up and says to him, 'Teacher, I will follow you wherever you might go.'" Jesus might have thought, as he would later say to the sons of Zebedee, "You do not know what you are asking" (Matt 20:22). For it is clear where Jesus goes. He goes to the other side and back again. Wherever he goes there are crowds or demoniacs or people following him and making requests of him. He is continually on the move.

That is what it means for Jesus to "go," and even the scribe who says he'll follow him wherever he goes makes his going rough. With all this movement, "The son of man," he warns the scribe, "has nowhere to lay his head" (Matt 8:20).

The scribe called Jesus "Teacher." Scribes, like monastics, are accustomed to domestic settings with scrolls, writing desks, and some leisure for personal study and meaningful conversations. The role the scribe assigns to Jesus, "Teacher," fits perfectly into the scribe's own world. Scribes and teachers belong to the same cultural environment, ordered, structured, predictable, and clean. Who do people say the Son of Man is? The scribe answers, "He is Teacher."

Teachers have places to lay their heads. Maybe they even lay their heads on their lecture podiums or on their desks.

But Jesus distances himself from this domestic scholarly role. He puts himself instead in the company of wild nature, foxes and birds, the open sky and the dark places of the earth. And even if foxes have holes and birds have nests, "the son of man has nowhere to lay his head" (Matt 8:20). Jesus made his home in Capernaum, but Matthew never says that he laid his head there (Matt 4:13; #1). In fact, you never read in the gospels about Jesus laying his head at all, except once, and that place only serves to throw into relief the truth of what Jesus said.[1]

It is in John's gospel, and it is when Jesus is on the cross: "When Jesus had received the vinegar, he said, 'It is finished'; and he bowed [literally, "laid"] his head" (John 19:30).

So true is it that the Son of Man has nowhere to lay his head that it is only when all is finished, on the cross, in the act of dying, that Jesus can finally "lay his head."

But even that is not the end. It continues, "He gave up his spirit." That is the end (John 19:30).

The scribe would not have understood all of this as clearly as we are able to, but he would have understood it to some degree. Following Jesus is not working on a Master's degree in theology. There is in fact something horrible about it.

After the scribe someone else comes, described as "another of the disciples" (Matt 8:21). A disciple is even more in the world of scribe and teacher. A disciple is one who learns, an apprentice, and so you cannot have a disciple without a teacher, without a master.

This disciple addresses Jesus, "Lord." He probably is not using the divine name but a title of respect, as a pupil in school might

---

1. Matthew tells us (Matt 8:24) that Jesus was sleeping in a boat. It is reasonable to assume that he laid his head when he slept. But Matthew, who just reported (Matt 8:20) Jesus saying that he had nowhere to lay his head, is consistent with his report by not saying that Jesus laid his head when he slept in the boat. The fact that he does not say that Jesus lays his head in the boat serves to emphasize the truth that Jesus has nowhere to lay his head. Luke says that Mary laid the newborn Jesus in a manger (Luke 2:7). Even if Jesus counted his infant self as the Son of Man, it was Mary who laid him, and not he who laid his head, and a manger, like a fox's hole and a bird's nest, is with respect to a human being nowhere.

have once addressed the professor as "sir." "Sir, let me first go and bury my father," that is, before I continue in your class.

Jesus' reply to this disciple is shocking. Jesus says a lot of jarring things, but this reply caps them all: "Follow me and let the dead bury their own dead." Origen remarks that to some this reply seems inhumane.[2] Undoubtedly it would have seemed so to Moses, and to God for whom he spoke. Moses granted military deferments to newlyweds and to people who had just built a new house, and even to the fearful and weakhearted (Deut 20:5-8). Jesus' kingdom-campaign has an unprecedented urgency.

If the disciple took this literally, then Jesus is telling the disciple to violate the fourth commandment, the one about honoring your mother and your father, a commandment that it was a point of the highest honor to fulfill.

I think Jesus *does* mean this literally, but only because he means it figuratively: Your father and all your people are dead, Jesus is saying, even if they are alive; dead because they don't follow me. "The gate is narrow and the way is hard that leads to life," he had said, "and those who find it are few" (Matt 7:14).

The only permissibly valid reason for breaking the commandment of God is the first part of Jesus' reply to the disciple, "Follow me." In Luke's version of this saying Jesus concludes with what must be Jesus' own interpretation: "No one putting his hand to the plow but looking at the things behind him is fit for the kingdom of God" (Luke 9:62).

I would say that monastic life is a narrow gate. We should take Jesus at his word—"those who find it are few"—and far from being disappointed or discouraged that "no vocations come," or that so many who come end up leaving, we should stand in awe that we and our brothers are here at all for all these years, in awe and gratitude.

Then, as people continuing along the narrow way sometimes in spite of ourselves, we can appropriate the spiritual interpretation

2. See Fragment 161 (ACCS 1a:167).

offered by Origen, who channels Saint Paul: Let the dead bury their dead means "Waste no more time on dead things. You are to 'put to death therefore what is earthly in you: immorality, impurity, passion, evil desire and covetousness, which is idolatry'" (see Col 3:5).[3]

So says the Teacher, the Lord, the one who finally laid his head in death, then breathed his spirit upon and within us so that we are as he is in this world.

3. See Fragment 161 (ACCS 1a:167).

35

On Matthew 8:23-26

(Mark 4:35-41; Luke 8:22-25)

We have been reflecting on the gospel of Matthew and are in chapter eight. At the sight of great crowds Jesus decided to go to the other side of the Sea of Galilee but was detained by two people, a scribe and a disciple. They gave Jesus the opportunity to say something about what it means to follow him: you'll risk having nowhere to lay your head, and not only will you break with your family, you'll also end up breaking one of the commandments and maybe more—"Follow me and let the dead bury their own dead" (Matt 8:18-22; #34).

So now Jesus does what he had started to do before the interruptions: he gets into the boat (Matt 8:23).

"And behold, there occurred a great storm on the sea so that the boat was being covered by the waves, but he was sleeping" (Matt 8:24). The "behold" tells us that the storm was a surprise. It's hard to believe that they would have set out on the sea if they had observed a storm brewing. They were adept at reading the signs of nature. They did not expect a storm right then.

Even so, the storm happening at that moment was no accident. It was Jesus on the sea that caused the great storm.

The sea is the forces of chaos, of death, and of the netherworld. The sea is the realm of what we heard at Vigils last Friday from Ephesians, not flesh and blood, not wind and rain only, but "the principalities, . . . the powers . . . of this present darkness, . . . [and] the spirits of evil in the heavens" (Eph 6:12). Jesus and his kingdom Gospel are a mortal threat to these powers.

The boat that Jesus with his disciples is in is covered by the water. The boat is the church struggling against the "gates of Hades" that Jesus will assure Peter will not prevail against it (Matt 16:18; #29).

Or, rather, it seems that the struggle is over. The boat being covered by the forces of death sure looks as though it's already been prevailed against, like the corpse of a monk dead now after a prolonged illness, after the hours consumed by gasping for life-breath have yielded at last to stillness.

How the disciples do what they do submerged in the sea we probably shouldn't spend too much time trying to figure out; the how is not the point: they "raise" Jesus and pray, "Save us, Lord, we are being destroyed" (Matt 8:25). Their prayer is a psalm reduced to its essentials, everything necessary intact.

Destruction is final. Destruction is the end the hostile cosmic powers have in mind for Jesus and the church, just as it will be the end the Pharisees intend when later they take "counsel against him how to destroy" Jesus (Matt 12:14).

When earlier in the gospel Jesus was baptized, Matthew wrote, "he immediately came up from the water." In his baptism, Jesus had been covered with water, just as he and the boat are covered with water now. In the boat, Jesus is asleep under the waters of destruction. In other words, he is (metaphorically) dead. So we need to give a lot of the weight to the disciples' action of *raising* him.

This scene is a death and resurrection account applicable to the entire church of every time, and to local churches and to disciples as well, like our monastic community, the church of New Melleray, and each of us individually.

The disciples have just heard the centurion plead with Jesus, "Lord, only say the word and my boy will be healed" (Matt 8:8; #31), and Jesus said that not even in Israel had he seen such faith as that man had (Matt 8:10). But in response to the disciples' raising Jesus from his sleep, invoking him as *Lord*, and praying that he save *them*, he says to them, "Why are you being cowards, O you small-of-faith?" (Matt 8:26).

Matthew does not give us the disciples' response to this rebuke, but we can imagine that they were puzzled, which is an intellectual response, and also hurt, which is a feeling response when people don't behave the way we have good reason to think they will. "Why did he call us *cowards* when *we* called him *Lord* and prayed that he *save us* from destruction? He *praised* that centurion for doing the same thing." Should the church *not* pray, "Lord, save us, we are being destroyed," when she finds herself under siege of mortal threat?

So maybe we need to read the story of the storm at sea as a catechesis on the postresurrection church and in light of the very last words of Matthew's gospel, "And look, I, I am with you"—that is, Emmanuel—"all days until the end of the age" (Matt 28:20; see Matt 1:23).

As he is now, Jesus is fully present in the church in his Word, in the ordained ministers, and not least in the liturgical assembly, the People of God, his Body. He is present body and blood, soul and divinity, present but veiled, submerged—under the appearances of bread and wine, as we say—in the Eucharist.

"The righteousness based on faith says, 'Do not say in your heart, "who will ascend into heaven" . . . to bring Christ down, or, "Who will descend into the abyss" to bring Christ up from the dead'" (Rom 10:6-7). Far from any need for us any longer to raise Christ, "we know," as Paul wrote, "that Christ being raised from the dead will never die again; death no longer has dominion over him" (Rom 6:9). "He is able for all time to save those who draw near to God through him, since he always lives to make intercession for them" (Heb 7:25).

"Then," in the very place where there occurred a *great storm*, "he arose and rebuked the winds and the sea, and there occurred a *great calm*" (Matt 8:26). Where the Risen Lord is, the great calm is the perduring inner reality at the heart of every destroying storm. This is how Saint Paul put the matter: "If Christ has not been raised, your faith is futile and . . . those who have fallen asleep in Christ have [already] been destroyed. If for *this life only* we have hoped in Christ, we are of all men most to be pitied" (1 Cor 15:17-19).

Later in the gospel of Matthew there is a very similar scene (Matt 14:24-31). This time, though, the Lord is not asleep under the sea of destruction but striding over it. Peter the Rock sinks and cries out, as the disciples do in the present scene, "Lord, save me," and Jesus says, as he does today, "O you small-of-faith, why did you doubt?" And at the very end of Matthew's gospel when the Eleven see the Risen Lord they worship him, but they also doubt (Matt 28:17).

Jesus allows in the church until the end of time this duality of faith and doubt, and so he calls his disciple "you small-of-faith." In Greek it's a single word, and only Jesus ever uses it, and then only for his disciples. Jesus can say that the Canaanite woman has "great faith" (Matt 15:28), and he can say that "this generation" is "faithless" (Matt 17:7), but he reserves "small-of-faith" for us. It is Jesus' word of endearment for us, like "children" in John (John 21:5) or "little flock" in Luke ("do not be afraid, little flock" [Luke 12:32]). Jesus knows that the realities of the kingdom—its nearness and light, its promised blessedness as well as its collateral horror—are too much for us to bear without the relief of faithful doubt even as we prostrate in worship before him.

36

On Matthew 8:28–9:1

(Mark 5:1-21; Luke 8:26-40)

Finally Jesus arrives at the other side of the Sea of Galilee (see Matt 8:18; #34). Jesus started to the other side when he saw great crowds around him. The impression is that he wanted to go to the other side to get away from those great crowds. Did he suppose that on the other side, it being pagan territory, nobody would have been interested in this itinerant Jewish rabbi and healer, if they'd even have heard of him, and that he would have a moment of peace?

If that was the case, Jesus was mistaken, and after a dramatic incident that involves two demon-possessed men, the demons themselves, a herd of pigs, the herdsmen, and the population of an entire city, Jesus got into the boat again and returned to where he started from. There is no getting away, no escape, no peace, at least not yet, for Jesus, for it is "the fullness of time" (Gal 4:4).

But as we learn, escaping was not the reason Jesus wanted to cross over. He crossed over for a purpose, accomplished the purpose, and then returned to his own city (Matt 9:1). Jesus had just told someone, "Let the dead bury their own dead," and then he was metaphorically dead himself, buried under the raging sea from which he was raised (Matt 8:21, 24, 25; see #34, #35). Now, arrived at the other side, two denizens of The Tombs, the place where the dead are buried, came out from there to meet him.

The Tombs sounds like the name of a neighborhood, like K-Town, Hell's Kitchen, the Tenderloin, and Back of the Yards. It is a place you don't want to go through even in daylight, and so Matthew says about The Tombs, "No one could pass that way" (Matt 8:28). The Tombs was occupied territory, gang controlled, and the gang's name was The Demons. Jesus is on their turf, The Tombs, and two members of The Demons come out to meet him.

This is where we, and maybe Jesus too, learn why Jesus came here "to the other side." The two demons tell us that when they ask Jesus, "Have you come here to torment us before the time?" (Matt 8:29). The story that we considered last week (#35) was Jesus provoking a battle with death and the cosmic powers symbolized by the event of a storm at sea. In this story he provokes the same powers in the human dimension. Just as "Behold, a great storm arose" in response to Jesus' setting out upon the sea on a boat, so now his mere presence on the other side provokes these demons to come out to meet him. "What have you to do with us, O Son of God?"

This is a showdown. They know whom they are dealing with long before Peter and the disciples will. This is not John's gospel. Jesus does not need maternal prompting to anticipate his hour (see John 2:2). It *is* before the time, but Jesus with his advent and his preaching of the kingdom's being near overwhelms decorum and annihilates eschatological certainties. Jesus has introduced a new time—the kingdom *Kairos*—not the Common Era but, as history has always affirmed, the *year of the Lord*, the acceptable time (see 2 Cor 6:2). Jesus has passed to the other side for no other reason than to purge The Tombs of The Demons who claimed it, because the kingdom brooks no delay.

The demons say to Jesus the same thing Jesus said to his mother at the wedding in Cana (Matt 8:29; see John 2:4). It's not a question so much as a provocation or even a dismissal. But I think this is a good thing for Christians to meditate on and present to Jesus as a real question: "What do we have to do with each other, you and me, Jesus, Son of God?" It is a form of Jesus' own question,

"Who do you say that I am?" (Matt 16:15). Who is Jesus to me? What am I to Jesus that he should care about me?

The demons know the terms of battle, and they know they've not a chance. As if praying, they "keep begging" Jesus, resigned to their fate, "if you cast us out," as they know he'll do.

But they also take a final jab at his whole new program of assembling disciples and sending them: "send us into the herd of swine," the word *send* being Jesus' way of commissioning his apostles (*apostellō*; Matt 8:31; see Matt 10:5).

Jesus' arrival provokes the demons to beg for their own demise. In this entire story loud with drama Jesus says only one word: addressing the demons he says to them, "Go!"

For the rest he is silent.

As leaders have done for every mobilized army anywhere in human history, the Romans supplied their occupying troops with brothels. The Roman soldiers' degrading term for these dehumanized women that their system turned into standard-issue prostitutes was *swine*. By association, the occupied local population applied the term to the troops themselves. So the astonishing scene of the herd of pigs rushing down the bank to drown in the sea like lemmings is more than Christian slapstick. It is a politico-eschatological double play on the part of Jesus.

From the prophet Daniel through Saint Paul to the Apocalypse of John, it is a fact that the "powers" and the "principalities" and the "world rulers of this present darkness" (Eph 5:12) always take up residence not just in human persons but in human structures and institutions, especially structures of oppressive power (see, e.g., Dan 7, Rev 17). So the fate of the pigs was at the same time both the Messianic defeat of those forces and the defeat in symbol of empire and its unjust and abusive ways. The drowning of the pigs—the demonic apostles—in the sea is a grotesque parody of Jesus and his disciples covered by the waves of the same sea in the scene we considered earlier, but the pigs and the powers really die, while Jesus was raised to bring the disciples to safety and calm (Matt 8:23-26; #35).

"The swineherds fled, and entering the city they announced everything, including the things about the demons" (Matt 8:33). It reminds you of Mary Magdalene and the women on Easter Sunday, and of the disciples of Emmaus that evening, running back and announcing—*apangellō*—everything (John 20:18; Luke 24:33-35). If the demons being sent were mock apostles, the swineherds become quasi-evangelists.

The word Matthew uses for what they do means to be an announcing angel (see Matt 1:20). It was truly good news, what happened, except, of course, if your livelihood depended on those pigs, and probably many people's did in one way or another; or if, however dangerous they were, The Demons patrolling from the neighborhood of The Tombs lent a kind of prestige and also tended to keep things safe, even at a price. "So the whole town came out to meet Jesus" (Matt 8:34).

Here at the end, the townspeople repeat exactly what the demons had done at the beginning: they go out to meet Jesus. But differently from the possessed men, they are not changed by meeting the Messiah. On the contrary, "and when they saw him they begged him to leave their district" (Matt 8:34).

Then, "he entered the boat, made the crossing, and came into his own town" (Matt 9:1).

This is one of the saddest passages in the gospels, all the more poignant and sorrow inducing because of Jesus' silence. But what could he have said? The swineherds had announced everything, like Mary and the women after the Resurrection (see Matt 28:8), like Paul in the Areopagus (Acts 17:22-34), like Bernadette at Lourdes, but those who heard begged him to leave their district. And he did.

But he had the satisfaction of knowing that he had done what he had come to do: come to torment before the time.

Is Jesus silent to us? Does his silence mean he is not here? As we move forward into a new and probably different chapter of our history as a community, as a church, shall we ask, "What do you have to do with us, Son of God?"

Who or what are the messengers and apostles of the Good News for us now before the time? Do we hear them? What structures of security, what identity markers, what interlocking and codependent patterns of relationships and behaviors in the life of a monastic community, of a family, of a parish, might be overthrown, collapse, unravel, and fall if we ask, "What do you have to do with us, Son of God?" and he tells us?

37

On Matthew 9:1-8

(Mark 2:1-12; Luke 5:17-26)

Even before Jesus was born his life was prearranged and preannounced. It was all in his name: "she will bear a son, and you shall call his name Jesus, for he will save his people from their sins" (Matt 1:21).[1] The angel Gabriel was developing the doctrine of the prophet Isaiah, who had said that they would call his name Emmanuel, which means "God is with us" (Isa 8:8; Matt 1:23).

Jesus is God with us, and the way God is most with us is in the forgiveness of sins. Jesus "embodies God's will not to allow sinful human beings to perish."[2] The adult Jesus himself confirms that he accepts and understands his life given him in his name before he was born. When finally he has come, he says why he came: "For I came not to call the righteous, but sinners" (Matt 9:13).

When Jesus arrives back to his own city after his visit to The Tombs, "they bring him a paralytic lying on his bed" (Matt 9:2). "They" are not identified, either by sex or number or in any other way except that they have faith: "Jesus saw their faith" (Matt 9:2).

---

1. See Karl Barth, *Dogmatics in Outline* (New York: Harper, 1959), 73: "This name and this title [Jesus Christ] express something . . .: they are a *revelation.*"

2. Reinhard Feldmeier and Hermann Spieckermann, *God of the Living: A Biblical Theology* (Waco: Baylor University Press, 2011), 319.

Jesus is sensitive to the presence of faith, and to its absence. The centurion had faith that amazed Jesus (Matt 8:10), and Jesus called the disciples in the boat "small-of-faith" (8:26). The faith of the people who bring the paralytic to Jesus is visible to him. Maybe the mere fact of bringing the paralyzed man to Jesus is their faith in action. Or maybe Jesus sees the fidelity of friends who would go to these lengths for their friend, in contrast to Job's friends who before God were embarrassed and scandalized by Job's misfortune.

In any case, it is his seeing their faith, or their faithfulness, that moved Jesus to say, "Courage, child, your sins are forgiven" (Matt 9:2). These are a prophet's words to God's people in distress: "Take courage, my children. . . . The one who has brought disaster upon you will, in saving you, bring you eternal joy" (Bar 4:26-29).

We can be certain of the connection between Jesus' response and the faith that he saw because on the same day, shortly after this, Jesus will say to a woman with a hemorrhage, "Courage, daughter, your faith has saved you" (Matt 9:22).

Furthermore, the similarity of these two words, "Courage, daughter, your faith has saved you" and "Courage, child, your sins are forgiven," affirms what we just said, that Jesus came to save his people from their sins. Christian salvation is the forgiveness of sins. It takes courage to receive this salvation, as Jesus also shows, because forgiveness and salvation necessarily issue in a new way of living, such as, "Be perfect, as your heavenly Father is perfect," which perfection is shown in loving our enemies (Matt 5:48, 44).

Forgiveness and salvation are the death of the old self and the creation of the new self. How will people recognize us if we are not paralyzed anymore or hemorrhaging anymore? How will we recognize ourselves? But the person who has been saved through faith and the forgiveness of sins is rightly claimed by Jesus as his own child, his son and daughter, because, as Saint Paul will say— and as we have seen—it is in Jesus that his or her life is now hidden, in God (Col 3:3; #22). In saving and forgiving, Jesus embraces each one into his own familial orbit. That orbit is what he calls "my church" (Matt 16:18), the sphere embracing those he has called.

Some scribes who were there thought that Jesus was blaspheming, but Jesus had not said, "I forgive your sins"; he said, "Your sins are forgiven." The passive voice makes it clear that God is the real subject of the verb "forgive." Jesus is being completely orthodox. Only God can forgive sins; this is what Jesus said.

To the paralyzed man, though, and to the people whose faith Jesus saw in their bringing him, Jesus' response must have seemed incongruous. Undoubtedly they expected him to cure the paralyzed man.

But for Jesus to say, "Your sins are forgiven" was not incongruous at all but just the opposite. In a sense it was the only thing Jesus, who came to call sinners and save his people from their sins, ever could have said and ever did say.

"This man is blaspheming," the scribes said to themselves, and "Jesus knew what they were thinking" (Matt 9:4). Jesus knows their thoughts not because he is a mind reader but because he is a Jew. Both Jesus and the scribes knew that "God's willingness to forgive . . . is anchored deep in God himself. Forgiveness is a behavior that is essential to God"; forgiveness is "the central experience of God's kindness and love," his *chesed* (see #39), which seeks in its turn "to awaken the response of reverent love" in the person and people God forgives.[3]

In spite of questions of grammar, Jesus knew very well that in saying, "Your sins are forgiven," he was saying that "the Son of man has authority on earth to forgive sins" (Matt 9:6), and he knew that the scribes knew it, too. They all knew that it was indeed blasphemy for Jesus to proclaim that God's readiness to forgive is displayed in his presence, that where he, the Son, is, the Father's forgiveness and salvation are available; "the unity of Father and Son" is expressed "in caring attention for sinners."[4]

Jesus' presence provoked the sea's rage (#35) and the demons' aggressive confrontation (#36). In a similar way, his presence effects

3. See Feldmeier and Spieckermann, *God of the Living*, 315, 318.
4. See Feldmeier and Spieckermann, *God of the Living*, 320.

forgiveness in response to evident faith. He knows that where he is, there is forgiveness, even when forgiveness is not what people think they need. The man, after all, was sick, paralyzed. But Jesus will go on to say in the same breath that it is the sick who need a physician and that "I came . . . to call sinners" (Matt 9:12, 13).

Nothing can better manifest the inner illness of sin than the outer illness of paralysis. We know how sin overwhelms our liberty and totally paralyzes our vital forces.[5] We lose spontaneity and joy. So Jesus does what the faithful companions of the sick man hoped for: "Rise, take up your bed, and go home" (Matt 9:6).

The crowds "saw this" (Matt 9:8). Matthew notes this fact, and we recall that Jesus "saw" the faith of the friends who brought the paralytic to him. By contrast, Matthew does not say that the scribes saw. If the scribes because they did not see were scandalized at Jesus' appropriation of divine authority to forgive sins, the crowds when they "saw" "were afraid and glorified God who had given such authority to men" (Matt 9:8).

You cannot help but think of the *sensus fidelium*, the felt understanding of the faithful that is often ahead of the curve in identifying what is true. And in fact soon in the gospel of Matthew Jesus will give his disciples "authority" "to drive out" "unclean spirits" "and to cure every disease and every illness" (Matt 10:1).

The man "rose and went home" (Matt 9:6). It was forgiveness in motion. But more than that, or rather that in other words, it was resurrection: "Rise," said Jesus, who himself had been raised from the death of sleep on the sea (Matt 8:25; #35), and his child, sustained by faith, took courage, and arose.[6] The crowd's response—they "were afraid and glorified God"—foreshadowed that of the women who will run from the empty tomb with fear and great joy (Matt 28:9), two profound religious feelings.

5. See Jean Radermakers, *Lettura Pastorale del Vangelo di Matteo* (Bologna: Dehoniane, 1972), 177.

6. See Radermakers, *Lettura Pastorale*, 177.

38

On Matthew 9:9-13

(Mark 2:13-17; Luke 5:27-32)

For Judaism even at the time of Jesus, in the words of New Testament scholar Ben F. Meyer, "The distinctions of clean and unclean and of righteous and sinners shaped and permeated the self-understanding of Judaism. To subvert these distinctions was not a breach of religious etiquette but a challenge to the social order." The clear distinction between the clean and the unclean was "a deeply rooted principle": "the absolute incompatibility of good and evil."[1]

Saint Paul understands himself according to these distinctions. Paul says in Galatians that he "progressed in Judaism beyond many of my contemporaries" (Gal 1:14), and in Philippians he affirms that he lived as "a Hebrew of Hebrews, in observance of the law a Pharisee . . . [and] blameless" (Phil 3:5, 6). As a Pharisee and devotee of Torah Paul would have known and supported the word of the prophet Nahum, "the Lord will not leave the guilty unpunished" (Nah 1:3), echoed by the Book of Proverbs: "Whoever acquits the wicked [is] an abomination to the Lord" (Prov 17:15).

So you should be bowled over when you hear Paul say, as he does in Romans, that when Abraham believed God, he believed in "the one who justifies the ungodly," even before any question of repentance on their part (Rom 4:5).

---

1. Ben F. Meyer, *The Aims of Jesus* (London: SCM, 1979), 159, 160.

It was no longer to be a righteousness of one's own based on Torah, but "the righteousness of God that depends on faith" in Christ (Phil 3:9).

Something must have happened to Paul the Pharisee, and we know that what happened was Jesus and the Gospel, concretized in what Meyer calls Jesus' "revolutionary contact and communion with sinners." In a world where sinners stood unquestionably condemned, "Jesus' openness to them was irresistible. Contact triggered repentance; conversion flowed from communion."[2]

Yesterday was the Feast of Saint Matthew. The gospel for the day was from the gospel of Matthew. It recounted the calling by Jesus of Matthew the tax collector, "Follow me," and how as Jesus "sat at table in the house, behold, many tax collectors and sinners came and sat down with Jesus and his disciples" (Matt 9:9, 10).

This is the second time Jesus has told someone to follow him, the other time being his words to the man who wanted to bury his father first (Matt 8:22; #34).

But, you might ask, what about Simon and Andrew, and James and John (Matt 4:18-22; #5)? Jesus told Simon and Andrew, "Come after me." In the case of James and John, Matthew just says, "He called them."

It is true that in terms of discourse, both "follow me" addressed to the tax collector Matthew, and "come after me" addressed to Simon and Andrew, are directive commands; there is no doubt about what is being asked. What is there not to understand?

It is a little different with "He called them," that is, James and John. There is no command, there is no direction. It is at the least a drawing of attention and at the most an open-ended invitation—but to what?

In any case, Peter and Andrew and James and John all got the point. They responded to the call of Jesus by following him. They understood what he intended and found in his call a real vocation.

2. Meyer, *The Aims of Jesus*, 160, 161.

As for Matthew the tax collector, he didn't just follow Jesus; he "rose and followed" Jesus (Matt 9:9). The paralytic last week "rose and went home" (Matt 9:7; #37), Peter's mother-in-law "rose and served him" (Matt 8:15; #32), and Jesus himself during the storm on the sea "rose and rebuked the winds" (Matt 8:26; #35). We are in the new age; it is resurrection life even in this mortal life doomed to death. This is the Gospel. This is the good news. What do we think we are doing every morning when we rise for Vigils? What does it mean for a Christian, and especially for a monk, to rise?

Matthew followed Jesus. Where to? "And it happened when he was at table in the house" (Matt 9:10). Our translation at Mass yesterday said, "his house," but the Greek of Matthew says just "the house." Saint Mark wrote "his house" (Mark 2:15), but that doesn't help. We naturally ask, "Whose house?" It could be Matthew's or Jesus'.

Maybe Saint Luke solves the problem: "Levi [who is Matthew by another name] made him a great feast in his house" (Luke 5:29). Clearly, for Luke, it is Levi's/Matthew's house in which Levi/Matthew made the feast for Jesus.

But we are reading Matthew, and he just says, "the house."

The natural conclusion is that it is Jesus' house. First, Matthew made it a point to say that Jesus came to his own city (Matt 9:1), so we would expect that he had a house there; or it could be Peter's house, where we saw that Jesus already felt at home (Matt 8:14). Second, Matthew is following Jesus. When you follow someone, you don't expect that person to lead you to your own house, but to their house or to someone else's, in this case, Jesus' house, or the house where Jesus is staying.

But I think asking if it was Matthew's house or Jesus' house misses the point. Matthew says, "the house," just as he says, "the boat." The house and the boat are almost like characters in the Gospel. The house is the place of intimacy and of being with Jesus in a semi-exclusive way.

In reality, the house is the church of every time and place. It is this community of New Melleray (see #32).

Especially, since it is *sitting down* in the house "with Jesus and his disciples," we understand the scene to be the eucharistic meal, the Mass, the commemoration through time of the Lord's Supper.

Later in the gospel of Matthew Jesus himself repeats what people were saying about his being "a glutton and a drunkard, a friend of tax collectors and sinners" (Matt 11:19). Jesus does not deny the charge, and the scene we are considering today is proof of it: "many tax collectors and sinners came and sat [at table] with Jesus and his disciples" (Matt 9:11; see verse 10). Ben Meyer says about this scene, "To his contemporaries it was a staggering phenomenon that [Jesus] did not shrink from dining with the irreligious." The religious reacted with shock and resentment (Matt 11:19), the irreligious with sheer delight (Luke 19:9).[3]

What Jesus was doing was more than the 351st footnote in a very long papal exhortation.[4] To the Pharisees Jesus was giving real scandal, that is, leading people to believe was true what was not true. "When the Pharisees saw this, they said to the disciples, 'Why does your teacher eat with tax collectors and sinners?'" (9:11).

The Pharisees see, and so they ask, "Why?" It is possible for us not to see at all, like the scribes in the passage we saw last week (#37). It is also possible to see but stop there, fail to ask "What" or "Why," and rush to judgment. The Pharisees both see and ask "Why?"

Giving them the benefit of the doubt, as we should, the Pharisees are trying to release the tension of scandal Jesus' action caused within them by seeking to understand. They are opening themselves to the joy of discovery, the joy of the Gospel. Presenting their question to the disciples, they are giving the church a golden opportunity to "give an explanation to anyone who asks you for a reason for your hope" (1 Pet 3:15).

3. Meyer, *The Aims of Jesus*, 158, 159.

4. The reference is to the controversy over that footnote in Pope Francis's *Amoris Laetitia*.

It is not the disciples who answer, though, but Jesus, as we will see next time.

In the meantime, let us recall what we say at the beginning of Mass: "Let us acknowledge our sins and so prepare ourselves to celebrate the sacred mysteries." Assembled in the church at Mass, we are at table in the house with Jesus and his disciples. To be worthy to be there, worthy, that is, in the eyes of Jesus, we need to be sinners and tax collectors. That is what we are doing when we start by acknowledging our sins. It is sinners whom Jesus seeks out, sinners whom he calls, sinners for whom he has come.

Let us be sinners before him, and let us also, like him, welcome sinners to the table of our life with compassion and humility, and take the time, too, when it seems OK to do so, to ask, "Why? Tell me your story."

39

On Matthew 9:10-13

(Mark 2:15-17; Luke 5:29-32)

"Why does your teacher eat with tax collectors and sinners?" the Pharisees asked Jesus' disciples in the house to which Matthew had followed Jesus (Matt 9:11; #38).

The Pharisees show that they are keeping a critical distance from Jesus and his disciples because they say "your teacher." Jesus is not their—not "our"—teacher, nor even *the* teacher.

For Jesus himself, there is no such distancing. Jesus refers to himself as "*the* Teacher." He is the Teacher for everyone. It is a role that transcends questions of identity or politics or persuasion. He calls himself "the Teacher" precisely in the contest of a meal: "Go into the city to a certain man and tell him, 'The Teacher says, "My appointed time draws near; in your house I shall celebrate the Passover with my disciples"'" (Matt 26:18).

So Jesus is not just "your teacher"; he is also "our teacher." Isaiah had said, "No longer will your Teacher hide himself, but with your own eyes you shall see your Teacher"; but the Pharisees didn't (Isa 30:20).

"Why does your teacher eat with tax collectors and sinners?" Matthew had said that "many tax collectors and sinners came and sat down with Jesus and his disciples" (Matt 9:10). Both Matthew and the Pharisees refer to the people at the table as collectives, not as individuals: tax collectors, sinners, and disciples; not

Matthew, Mary, and Peter. Collective titles are convenient: if there was a report about the Mass of Remembrance it might say, "Attending the Mass of Remembrance were mourners, monks, and Trappist Caskets employees."[1]

But we know that these collective labels are inadequate for anything beyond a brief report in a newspaper. Each member of these three collectives has a unique story. If you attended the Mass of Remembrance and then just stood there when Mass was over, individuals came up to you and told you their story. They came from particular places, and their deceased loved ones had names. Each of these stories is part of the history of grace; in a sense, each story is part of the glory of God that is the earth's fullness (Isa 6:3).

Luke tells of a woman who anointed Jesus' feet. She belonged to the collective "sinner" (Luke 7:37-38). "If this man were a prophet he would know what sort of woman this is . . . for she is a sinner," said the Pharisee who had invited him (Luke 7:39). But Jesus said in reply, "Do you see *this* woman?" That is, this particular woman, whom he then goes on to describe in terms of each of her particular actions that manifest her great love (Luke 7:44-47). Do you *see* this woman?

The Pharisees asked the disciples about their Teacher's practice of eating with tax collectors and sinners, a practice that as we saw last week (#38) was uniquely emblematic of who Jesus himself was and that caused a great deal of scandal. They asked "Why?" and we gave them credit for asking and not rushing to judgment on the mere basis of what they saw or heard.

They asked the disciples.

You wonder why—there's "Why?" again—why they did not ask Jesus himself. Was he too busy eating? Was he too busy listening to people? But it says that Jesus heard and that it was he and not the disciples who answered (Matt 9:12).

---

1. New Melleray holds an annual Mass in commemoration of all buried in the abbey's Trappist Caskets products in the previous year. It is attended by upwards of six hundred relatives and friends of the deceased.

If I had been Jesus I would have kept on listening to find out what my disciples would answer. Why did *they* think I ate with tax collectors and sinners? But Jesus answers the Pharisees himself, maybe to keep his disciples from embarrassment, maybe taking the opportunity as a good teacher always does to teach.

His answer is characteristically in the form of a parable. That means among other things that he is throwing the question back to the Pharisees to answer for themselves. If they are sincere in their asking "Why," they will take the time to get the sense of the parable Jesus tells them. Jesus does not teach like the Baltimore catechism, but more like the Catechism of John Paul II, which requires the personal engagement of the person using it. "Why?" they asked. Because, he answers, "the healthy have no need for a physician, but those who are sick" (Matt 9:13).

For a moment Jesus steps out of the role of teacher and takes on another, that of physician. As Matthew said earlier in chapter eight, Jesus the physician fulfilled what was spoken by the prophet Isaiah: "He took our infirmities and bore our diseases" (Matt 8:17).

"The healthy have no need for a physician, but those who are sick." You can reduce Jesus' answer to *I meet people in their need for me.* He is loving Jesus. That is why he eats with tax collectors and sinners. Like the tax collector and the Pharisee in the parable that Saint Luke reports, sinners know what they need; the righteous know only what they have (Luke 18:9-14).

Then, always the teacher, Jesus says, "Go and learn" (Matt 9:13a). "Go and learn what this means," Jesus says, and then quotes the prophet Hosea: "I desire mercy, not sacrifice" (Matt 9:13; Hos 6:6).

The Greek word for *mercy* normally means compassion or pity or even clemency: "Mother of Mercy, . . . O Clement Virgin Mary."[2] Here, though, the word *mercy* is a translation of *chesed* in the Hebrew of Hosea, and if we read that entire verse in Hosea a slightly different meaning of mercy is seen: "For it is *chesed* that I

---

2. The line is from the hymn *Salve, Regina,* which Cistercians sing at the closing of every day of their lives.

desire, not sacrifice; and knowledge of God rather than burnt offerings" (Hos 6:6).

The parallelism tells us that if "sacrifice" corresponds to "burnt offerings," then *chesed* or mercy is "knowledge of God" in other words, so with good reason Jesus said, "Go and learn." Mercy is an intimate familiarity with—knowledge of—God. To be merciful is to be in the truth.

Matthew is the only New Testament author who has Jesus quote this verse from Hosea, and Jesus quotes it twice, the other time in chapter twelve: "If you had known what it means, 'I desire mercy, not sacrifice,' you would not have condemned the guiltless" (Matt 12:7).

In chapter nine it is "Go and learn," and in chapter twelve, "If you had known." So in chapter twelve they had not yet acted on the teacher's instruction; they had *not* gone and learned. It is almost as if in chapter twelve it is too late to learn that mercy and not sacrifice is the object of divine desire, or, we might say, divine *eros*.

Whatever mercy is, at least it is for the sake not of pity, but of truth: to withhold damning judgment of the innocent, condemnation of the guiltless. And one of the first steps in coming to the truth is to suspect that you might be wrong, and so to ask "Why?" and "Is it true?"

Condemning the guiltless is a betrayal of your own ignorance, Jesus seems to be saying. In his magnificent sermon twelve on the Song of Songs Bernard describes the last of three ointments, the ointment of mercy. The first ointment is contrition, the second is devotion, but the third, mercy, far excels both of these (Bernard, SC 12.1; CF 4:77–78).

The ingredients of the ointment of mercy are "the manifold misfortunes of people of all classes who endure affliction, even if they are our enemies" (SC 12.1; CF 4:77). The person possessed of this ointment makes himself all things to all, ever ready to supply what they need, so dead to himself that he lives only for others (SC 12.1; CF 4:78). Mercy, says Bernard, "works for the welfare of the afflicted and is diffused through the whole Body of Christ," the body, that is, "that was acquired by his passion," the church and her members (SC 12.10; CF 4:85).

In this sermon Saint Bernard then quotes Matthew quoting Jesus quoting Hosea: "What I want is mercy, not sacrifice" (SC 12.10; CF 4:85). I will conclude with this memorable passage from Bernard's sermon twelve on mercy:

> And you, too, . . . if you are at all times courteous, friendly, agreeable, gentle and humble, you will find men everywhere bearing witness to the influence you radiate. Everyone among you who not only patiently endures the bodily and mental weaknesses of his neighbors, but, if permissible and possible, even plies them with attentions, inspires them with encouragement, helps them with advice, . . . assist[s] them by fervent prayers—everyone, I repeat, who performs such deeds among you, gives forth a good odor among the brothers like a rare and delicate perfume. . . . This is a man who loves his brothers, who prays much for [them]." (SC 12.5; CF 4:81–82)

I like it that Matthew's gospel ends with Jesus' great commission, "Go and make disciples," in Greek, *poreuthentes oun mathēteusate,* a fine correlative to "Go and learn," *poreuthentes de mathete* (Matt 28:19; Matt 9:13).

40

On Matthew 9:14-15

(Mark 2:18-20; Luke 5:33-35)

". . . on the day of his marriage, on the day of the joy of his heart" (Song 3:11). The day of marriage is a day of joy. We verify this fact even in our pretty joyless culture. We know that one of our employees and his fiancée have gone off to Colorado, where they will be married. Perhaps it was yesterday. It will have been a day of joy. They wanted the beauty of the Rockies to participate in the joy of their hearts. "As a bridegroom rejoices in his bride," it says of the Lord himself in the prophet Isaiah, and Raguel said to Tobiah at the time of Tobiah's marriage to Sarah, "For fourteen days you shall . . . eat and drink . . . and bring joy to my daughter's . . . spirit" (Isa 62:5; Tob 8:20).

We were just at a meal in the house to where Matthew followed Jesus (Matt 9:9-10; #38, #39). In the discussions there Jesus was a teacher and then a physician.

But it doesn't take long for the imagery to change again, and now Jesus is a bridegroom at a wedding. "Can the wedding guests mourn as long as the bridegroom is with them?" Jesus asks "the disciples of John" who had "approached him and said, 'Why do we and the Pharisees fast much, but your disciples do not fast?'" (Matt 9:14-15).

There has been no mention of a wedding in the gospel of Matthew so far, so the only way to explain Jesus' calling himself a bridegroom out of any literary context is the context of his own self-understanding. Jesus has just quoted from the prophet Hosea (Matt 9:13; Hos 6:6; #39). He is always in the thought world of that prophetic book whose currents of spousal love merge with those of the Song of Songs. Earlier in Hosea the Lord God, a bridegroom himself, said to his Beloved Israel, "I will betroth you to myself forever. . . . I will betroth you to myself in truth, and you shall know the Lord" (Hos 2:21, 22; see also #28 and #41).

In the story Matthew told about the centurion whose servant was sick, Jesus talked about people coming from east and west to "recline with Abraham, Isaac, and Jacob at the banquet of heaven" (Matt 8:11; see #31). Never far from Jesus' mind but rather always present is the fact of the kingdom of heaven's having come near so that it is not far but very close. The kingdom of God for Jesus as for the prophets and poets of Israel is best understood as a *convivium*, a banquet, a party, and in particular a wedding banquet, a marriage between God and his people.

Jesus never says so directly, but his allusions make it clear enough that he knows that he himself is the Bridegroom at the wedding. Wherever he is, there is the wedding banquet, and all the more is this true when it is an actual meal, as it was in the house to which Matthew had followed him, and ever after and everywhere after that in the church's eucharistic meals. It is already the time of fulfillment, and Jesus is the Messiah/Bridegroom of all expectation.

Jesus was way ahead of the writer of the Apocalypse, who, late in the game, summed it up when he wrote, "Blessed are those who are invited to the marriage supper of the Lamb" (Rev 19:9).

It was clear a moment ago that we were in the house and at a meal (Matt 9:10). Now, to tell the truth, it is not so clear where we are, even if the discussion is about eating or not eating. Matthew just says, "Then the disciples of John approached."

It may still be the same house, and if it is, it is a very open and inclusive environment, for not only are Jesus and his disciples there, and many tax collectors and sinners, and Pharisees; in addition, now there are disciples of John the Baptist, and in a minute an official will come and kneel before Jesus (Matt 9:18).

"Why do we and the Pharisees fast much but your disciples do not fast?" John's disciples ask.

Again we have the "Why" question (see Matt 9:11; #38, #39). Something has been observed, some data have been collected: we fast, the Pharisees fast, Jesus' disciples do not fast. As we have seen before, it would be easy enough to rush to judgment and conclude something about all these people on the basis of contrasts among them. But the disciples of John, like the Pharisees before them, understand that to come to a true judgment about someone you have to have some understanding about the matter. That is what the Why question is for.

We know that John the Baptist was an ascetic of some sort. We don't have to take his disciples' word for it that John fasted; Matthew told us that "his food was locusts and wild honey" (Matt 3:4), and Jesus will say, "John came neither eating nor drinking" (Matt 11:18).

And we know from the parable of the Pharisee and the publican in the gospel of Luke that Pharisees fasted: "I fast twice a week," he boasted to himself, and so did most of the Pharisees and other pious Jews (Luke 18:12).

When John's disciples ask Jesus, "Why do we and the Pharisees fast much but your disciples do not fast?" I don't think the "Why" is really about them or the Pharisees; they are not asking why *they* fast. They already know why; even if it is just out of cultural habit, that is still a reason. But they are setting themselves and the Pharisees up as a standard against which to understand and to decide about Jesus and his disciples.

They could just as well have asked—but themselves, not Jesus— "Hey, we notice that he and his disciples don't fast, so what are we and the Pharisees doing fasting so much?" That question could have led to an illuminating insight; it would have been the kind of self-reflective question that Jesus' parables and his way of life are trying to provoke in us all the time. But the disciples of John have not been so provoked yet, so they make themselves and the Pharisees the standards of righteous behavior: "Since we behave this way, what do you think you are doing behaving just the opposite?"

In fact we know that Jesus was not a stranger to fasting. He fasted forty days in the desert (Matt 4:2). Nor are his disciples, including us, strangers to fasting, for Jesus says, "When you fast" and even "Blessed are those who hunger and thirst for righteousness" (Matt 6:16; 5:6).

But here Jesus does not deny that he and his disciples do not fast; that is, he lets go without challenging it the claim that they don't as the grounds for his being accused of being "a glutton and a drunkard" (Matt 11:19).

Jesus did eat and drink with tax collectors and sinners, the company as much as the eating and drinking being signs of his relaxed attitude toward religious decorum. Why? He responds to a question with a question. In addition, as he did in the passage we looked at last week, when he said, "Those who are well have no need for a physician" (Matt 9:12; #39), he gives his reply the form of a parable: "The wedding guests can't mourn as long as the bridegroom is with them, can they?" (Matt 9:15).

Notice that Jesus' question is the kind that expects *No* for an answer. It is stating the obvious, and to answer *Yes* would be absurd. "Can wedding guests mourn as long as the bridegroom is with them?" "Of course not." So Jesus, clever teacher and physician of souls that he is, throws the question right back to the questioners, makes them answer it themselves and at the same time learn something both scandalous and productive of ecstatic joy: here and now is the Wedding Feast that our own fasting has made us blind to!

I have learned that I like to live in a world that I have created myself. I expect and even demand that others live in it, too. Mine, after all, is the real world, isn't it? Call it World M for Mine.

Jesus and his disciple live in World K for Kingdom, and the disciples of John and the Pharisees live in World F for Fear. Jesus will not let them co-opt *his* followers for *their* world. "While he is with them." Still, Jesus says, "the days will come when the bridegroom is taken away from them, and then they will fast" (Matt 9:15).

We note that in his little parable about the bridegroom Jesus has replaced *fast* in the question of John's disciples with "mourn." Doing that, Jesus gives a precise meaning to fasting: fasting is an act of mourning, and we mourn what is lost and gone forever, especially a person, a loved one. In the Sermon on the Mount Jesus said, "Blessed those who are mourning, for they shall be comforted," that is, by God (Matt 5:4).

Fasting, then, regards the past and determines my fundamental posture for the present: my fasting says that I am a mourner, but it also is a door of hope open to another realm, another power, a future fulfillment, the attainment of which is out of my hands.

Fasting reminds me that even in my loss, which I mourn, I am not alone in hope and aspiration. The Risen Lord says famously, "I am with you always, to the close of the age" (Matt 28:20), the very closing words of the gospel of Matthew.

So what does Jesus mean, *the days will come*, "when the bridegroom is taken away from them?"

He is referring of course to what we call the passion—to his arrest in Gethsemane, his death on Calvary, and his burial in the tomb.

But I think he is referring to more than that.

"The days will come," and they will keep coming. It is the time we live in, history, the temporal order, we might say, the time of the Body of Christ, the Church, subject to persecution. And so continually during *these days* that will *keep on coming till the end of the ages* the bridegroom is taken away.

That is why Saint Benedict follows Christian practice that goes back at least to the *Didache* (Did 8.1), when, in addition to the traditional Lenten fast, he says that outside of Easter time "monks fast until midafternoon on Wednesday and Friday" (RB 41.2), and every day from September 14 till the Lenten fast (RB 41.6).

These days that keep coming constitute a time for mourning a loss, the loss of the Bridegroom, but also the time of hope and aspiration that do not disappoint because, at the same time, "I am with you always, to the close of the age," the Bridegroom already at the Wedding Supper of the Lamb, where we join him in both fact and anticipation at every eucharistic gathering of fellow thieves, tax collectors, and sinners.

On the other hand, from the perspective of the New Wine (Matt 9:17; #41), Jesus in proclaiming that the kingdom of God was near and so not far, in celebrating with tax collectors and sinners at the wedding feast now, was doing nothing but fasting day and night. Very soon in Matthew disciples of John, maybe the same disciples who just approached him, will ask Jesus on John's behalf, "Are you the one who is to come?" (Matt 11:2-6). John in prison had heard tell of the "works of the Messiah." Jesus sends the disciples back with this word to John: "the blind regain their sight, the lame walk, lepers are cleansed . . . and the poor have the good news proclaimed to them." But what are these "works of the Messiah" if not what Isaiah already eight hundred years before had identified as "the *fast* I [the Lord] choose: releasing those bound unjustly, untying the thongs of the yoke, . . . sharing your bread with the hungry, bringing the afflicted and the homeless into your house" (Isa 58:6-7)? In these days when the Bridegroom has been taken away, his disciples, the ministering and martyred church, continue to fast in the same way, drunk with the New Wine and busy with the Works of Mercy.

41

On Matthew 9:16-17

(Mark 2:21-22; Luke 5:36-39)

"No one puts a piece of unshrunk cloth on an old garment" (Matt 9:16a). Is this a statement of divine truth, or of human practical economy? It sounds like something Jesus learned from Mary his mother rather than from his heavenly Father.

"No one." In fact there were and would continue to be people who patched old garments with unshrunk cloth if for no other reason than there being nothing else available; they'd have to take the chance.

So Jesus'—or his mother Mary's—saying is not a fact; it is a principle or a counsel. No wise person who had a choice in the matter would put a piece of unshrunk cloth on an old garment. Would people be sinning if they used the wrong cloth to patch an old garment, because then they would be violating a counsel of Jesus? Or would they just be weak in judgment or, again, lacking in alternatives? Does Jesus' statement have moral implications for us?

Would our answers be different if Jesus didn't mean to be taken literally but figuratively? What if his statement about patching an old garment was a parable? In that case Jesus might be stating a divine truth rather than giving a home economics lesson. For Jesus did speak in parables, and he framed his most important teachings in figures and allegories and stories.

Jesus goes on: if you do patch an old garment with unshrunk cloth, "the patch pulls away from the garment, and the tear ends up worse than ever" (Matt 9:16b).

Jesus presents us with a garment that is both old and torn. At the trial of Jesus the high priest will tear his garment when Jesus says that from then on they will "see the Son of Man . . . coming on the clouds of heaven" (Matt 26:64, 65). The high priest accompanies the tearing of his garment with an exclamation: "He has blasphemed" (Matt 26:65). His torn garment bears witness to his judgment that Jesus has blasphemed by proclaiming that the new messianic age that everyone knew was in an untouchable future was in fact here, and now.

Moths destroy garments. In the book of the prophet Hosea there is a moth. In this prophetic book God is the husband undyingly faithful in the face of persistent betrayal, Israel/Ephraim his promiscuous bride (see, e.g., Hos 2:21-25; 1:7-9). But at one point God is a moth, moth and rot, and Ephraim/Israel is the garment (Hos 5:12; see Ps 39:12). This uncanny image is, I think, the kind that especially would have inspired Jesus, as equally would have its redemption in the Song of Songs where the bride's garments are praised by the Bridegroom/God for being as fragrant as Lebanon (Song 4:11).

The high priest's garment is old and torn, in contrast to Jesus' own garment, which even during his earthly life had the properties of the Age to Come. In just a few verses from this parable about the old torn garment and the patch, a woman will touch the mere hem of Jesus' garment and be healed after twelve years of suffering, twelve signifying the Old Law of the Patriarchs (Matt 9:20; #42).

It is the same garment, Jesus', that will become white as light in the transfiguration (Matt 17:2). Jesus' garment is not torn. John's gospel makes a point of saying so (John 19:23). Even the heavens are torn and will all wear out like a garment, but God neither changes nor has an end (see Ps 102:27-28). He is ever ancient, ever new.

The old torn garment cannot receive the new patch. We have to know something about the making and properties of cloth to understand this, but it is true. The patch "pulls away." It is the same word Jesus had just used about the Bridegroom, who would be "taken away," and in that day they would fast, referring to both his coming passion and his post-ascension absence (Matt 9:15; #39).

Matthew uses the Greek word *plērōma* for patch. *Plērōma* means fullness: a patch fills a tear in a garment.

It is the only time Matthew uses this word, but Paul uses it several times and John once, but neither John nor Paul uses it to mean "patch." "From his fullness we have all received, grace upon grace" (John 1:16).

Jesus' entire garment is fullness; fullness is the energy and substance of his new, whole, eternal garment. Love is the fullness of the Law that was born of a woman in the fullness of time (Rom 13:10; Gal 4:4). In Christ all the fullness of divinity dwells bodily so that the Church, which is his Body, is the fullness of him who fills all things (Col 2:9; Eph 1:23).

It is no wonder that the fullness pulls away from the high priest's torn garment that so clings to the past as to call the presence of the future—now in your midst—blasphemy. The old garment cannot receive and accommodate the patch of the fullness, for then the tear would only become worse.

In Matthew's Greek, "tear" is *schisma*, the word we get *schism* from. It is the result of an act of tearing. When we first meet the future apostles James and John they are in their boat mending their nets (Matt 4:21). That means that the nets were torn. But after the resurrection, Peter drags a net ashore, and though it is full (*meston*) of large fish, the net is *not* torn (John 21:11).

"Let us not tear it," said the soldiers about Jesus' garment, the clothes of the Bridegroom on the cross, who right at that moment is being taken away (John 19:24). His untorn garment was his resurrection body in anticipation—more than restoration, the very fullness of God.

Jesus immediately tells another parable about wine and wineskins, making the same point (Matt 9:17).

Paul appeals to the Corinthians quite openly that there be no schisms among them, even though he hears reports that there are and half believes them (1 Cor 1:10; 11:18; 12:25). It is the church especially more than nets and garments that is susceptible to schisms, to splits and tears, and ultimately it is the church that Jesus and Matthew have in mind when they talk about torn garments and burst wineskins, the universal church and each local church, even a monastic church like ours. "That there be no schism in the body," says Paul, "but that the members have the same care for one another" (1 Cor 12:25).

A schism is calling blasphemy the presence of God's evernewness, a presence that must always seem blasphemous and scandalous to the self-righteous and the fearful.

And then as now, schism in the church is most sharply evident at the celebration of the Lord's Supper: accentuation of factions around separate allegiances, the elites and the powerless, the rich and the poor.

The church at its best and healthiest is when at the Eucharist, in the words of Fanny Howe, "there are sick, vomiting, maimed, screaming, destroyed, violent, useless, happy, pious, fraudulent, hypocritical, lying, thieving, hating, drunk, rich, poverty-stricken people," all together in the forgiveness and the peace of the fullness of Christ.[1]

Christ is the only patch that can repair breaches. Christ who makes all things new alone can renew and repair his church.

What about the renewal of the Cistercian Order, the revitalization of its individual communities? You could try putting an old patch on an old garment, say the patch of Rancé's La Trappe on the garment of 1970s optimism.[2] But eventually one or the other will falter and both will go down together.

---

1. Quoted in Anthony Domestico, "Saying the Unsayable," *Commonweal*, November 2019, 33.

2. The reference is to the Cistercian Abbey of La Trappe under abbot Armand Jean de Rancé (1629–1700), whose reforming efforts were decisive for the late-nineteenth-century creation of the Order of Cistercians of the Strict Observance, popularly known as "Trappists" after Rancé's abbey.

Or you could make entirely new wineskins to hold the New Wine so both will be preserved. What would new monastic wineskins look like, to hold the New Wine that is the fullness of Christ, the love that loves to the end?

Very concretely, it would look like manifest gestures of heartfelt forgiveness among us and celebrated at the Kiss of Peace and in a weekly *mandatum*, and with everyone in a personal and manifest way connected to the abbot, who holds the place of Christ, as to a hub.[3]

This is not just evangelical counsel; it has the breath of divine truth.

3. *Mandatum*—Latin, literally, "something enjoined or commanded." In Christian and monastic usage the *mandatum* is the mutual washing of feet after the example and command of Jesus (see John 13:14-15 and context; RB 35.9, 53.13). Once a weekly practice in Cistercian monasteries, the *mandatum* has pretty much been abandoned (in the Roman Rite the *mandatum* is performed after the homily in the Mass of the Lord's Supper on Thursday of Holy Week). At New Melleray I attempted to open the door to a revival of the *mandatum* there, proposing that for Saint Bernard the *mandatum* was a quasi sacrament, and that for Cistercians it is what might be called the extraordinary form of eucharistic adoration. See Olivier Quenardel, "La route du sel; Jalons pour une théologie de la vie cistercienne," Coll 79 (2017): 343–57, for the revival of the *mandatum* at the Abbey of Cîteaux, France.

42

On Matthew 9:18-26

(Mark 5:21–43; Luke 8:40–56)

Don't use old wineskins when it is a question of new wine; use new ones, and it is a question of new wine (Matt 9:17; #41).

Matthew follows the account of Jesus' parables about the patch and the garment and the wine and the wineskins with two stories about Jesus and females, one young and one apparently older. Matthew embeds one story within the other like wine in a flagon showing us that the two stories need each other.

Jesus is saying these things about the patch and the garment and the new wine and the wineskins when a certain official comes. It actually says "one official." The official worships Jesus and announces that his daughter has just died. "But," he continues, "come and put your hand upon her and she will live" (Matt 9:18).

This one official's announcement to and request of Jesus are made simultaneously with Jesus speaking his parables about the patch and the wineskins. The daughter has just died, literally, come to an end. She is like an old torn garment. "Come, lay your hand upon her"; but no one lays a patch of new cloth on an old garment or puts new wine in old skins. This official is pushing Jesus, challenging the implied promise of his parable: "You can repair the ruined garment; you can make my dead daughter live by giving her new wine."

The official "worships" Jesus. It is a spontaneous gesture on his part, probably not so much humble as just true, and really the most important of the three gestures he is said to have performed: "Coming, he worshiped him, saying." Earlier Jesus told Satan that he should worship God alone, and the magi do just that when they worship the child Jesus in Bethlehem (Matt 4:10; 2:11).

When the official says that his daughter has died and then says, "but come . . . and she will live," Jesus rises (Matt 9:19). In succession we hear the words *died, will live,* and *rising.* The entire Gospel and every part of it is the New Wine of the Resurrection, the unshrunk cloth, the untorn garment.

Then Jesus and his disciples follow the official, a twist, since it has been others who followed Jesus and his disciples, a twist not so much true as humble.

He had said, "She has just died, but come."

"But come."

"But." Isn't everything of the New Wine in that one word, *but?*

But is different from *so.* "Six-pack of Bud, eight dollars; jar of peanuts, two; so that'll be ten bucks."

But the Gospel's perspective is different, like Jesus following an official, a twist not reasonable—"these are the facts, so,"—but merciful—"these are the facts, but." "Six-pack of Bud, eight dollars; jar of peanuts, two; but, hey, it's Thanksgiving, right? Just have a good holiday."

The official's *but* is the difference between defeat and thriving, between death—she "just died"—and life—"she will live." *But* is the seamless garment, the new wineskin that is there to receive the New Wine. It is the faith that contains joy, the hope that invites participation.

What kind of people are we—*so* people, or *but* people, resigned to facts and their embedded fate, or inspired by mercy and grace?

"And rising, Jesus and his disciples followed him." The Risen Lord with his church is at the service of those whom the facts of death render helpless but not hopeless. In the *but* is the faith that constrains God to humble himself and follow. "Jesus followed . . . him," the twist that is the pattern of all ecclesial leadership, even monastic leadership; the leader following the led wherever their need will lead. It is the New Wine. It is loving Jesus.

Jesus follows, and someone comes up behind him, a woman hemorrhaging for twelve years. We can say that she is an old wineskin cracked and leaking. The official's daughter has just died; this woman is dying. But—"If I but touch his garment I will be saved" (Matt 9:21)—and she does touch it, silent as the dead can only be in relation to the living, touches his untorn garment, his resurrection body.

Maybe to the Jewish Christians Matthew wrote for, the twelve years of the woman's illness represented Israel with its twelve tribes, their Jewish heritage that was wasting away with nothing to stop the hemorrhaging except the secret unspoken thought, "If only I could touch his garment," God's very self, the garment of glory that filled the temple in Isaiah's vision (Isa 6:1, Hebrew).

"And coming from behind she touched the hem of his garment" (Matt 9:20).

Turning and seeing her, Jesus calls her "Daughter." If the bleeding woman is Israel, Jesus affirms her claim of divine election by adopting her as daughter: "I passed by and saw you struggling in your blood, and I said to you in your blood, 'Live'" (Ezek 16:6); "Awake, awake! Put on your strength, Zion, put on your glorious garments, Jerusalem, holy city. . . . Loose the bonds from your neck, captive daughter Zion! For thus says the Lord: For nothing you were sold, without money you shall be redeemed" (Isa 52:1-2).

So Jesus says to the woman, "Courage, daughter, your faith has saved you" (Matt 9:22). Saint Paul will say in Romans, "God is one and will justify the circumcised on the basis of faith and the uncircumcised through faith" (Rom 3:30). And the woman was saved from that very hour, cured in an instant in contrast to the twelve years of her life draining away.

Then Jesus comes to the official's house and finds the scene of mourning, a scene simultaneous with the rejoicing and festivity we can imagine around the woman who was just saved. It is the difference between a *so* mentality marked by commotion and a *but* mentality marked by silent waiting. Contradicting the official who said the daughter had died, and contradicting clinical fact, "She did not die; she is sleeping," says Jesus, while ordering the *so* population to "Go away." They do, with ridicule (Matt 9:24).

The clinical fact does not change, just the name given it, refusing to the fact the power to define itself: in the presence of Resurrection, death is sleep. Death is final; sleep is transitory and restorative.

"He came and took her by the hand, and the little girl arose" (Matt 9:25), and that is the Good News that continues to spread through the land (9:26), the New Wine flowing.

43

On Matthew 9:27-31

(see Mark 8:22-26)

In our ongoing commentary on the gospel of Matthew we have come to the story of the two blind men who followed Jesus shouting, "Have mercy on us, Son of David" (Matt 9:27-31). This story comes right after the intertwined accounts of the healing of the woman with a hemorrhage and of the raising to life of the official's daughter (Matt 9:18-26; #42).

I think we have to see all three of these stories, like the entire Gospel, under the umbrella of the earlier parable about the new wine and the new wineskins (Matt 9:16-17; #41). The Gospel brings restoration and unimagined splendor even as it threatens and brings about ruin and destruction. The new will always triumph over the old.

The men call Jesus "Son of David." The very first words of Matthew's gospel are "The book of the genealogy of Jesus Christ, the son of David" (Matt 1:1). We could translate that first phrase literally, the "Book of Genesis." Jesus is the absolute new beginning of creation; he is the new Adam, but he is also Son of David.

As Son of David Jesus is rooted in history, the history of Israel stretching from Abram of Ur to the kingdom of Herod under the Roman Empire. David is the chosen son of the Lord. Nothing says this better than Psalm 89. "I have chosen David my servant . . . . He shall cry to me, 'You are my father,' . . .; I myself make him my firstborn" (Ps 89:21, 27, 28; #16, #17).

And yet he is also the failed king. The Lord had said, "I will never be false to David. . . . His dynasty will continue forever" (Ps 89:36, 37), but, "Now you have rejected and spurned. . . . Where are your former mercies, Lord, that you swore to David in your faithfulness?" (Ps 89:39, 50).

From then on, David and the Son of David stood for the Messiah, for the definitive fidelity in history of the creating and redeeming God, fidelity to himself in his fidelity to his people. When the two blind men, and Matthew himself, and the Canaanite woman in chapter fifteen, and the crowds on the road between the Mount of Olives and Jerusalem shouting, "Blessed is he who comes in the name of the Lord" all call Jesus "Son of David," they are making a claim on God's fidelity to himself—"Where are your former mercies, Lord, that you swore to David in your faithfulness?" (Ps 89:50)—and expressing their own faith that God's faithful mercy is right there in the person of Jesus of Nazareth.

"Have mercy on us," the blind men plead, as will the Canaanite woman (Matt 15:22), recalling again Psalm 89, "I will sing of your mercy forever, Lord, your faithfulness through all ages."

In this magnificent, deeply honest, and moving Davidic Psalm 89, mercy (*chesed*; see #18, #39) and faithfulness are the Lord's motivations for and the sources of all he does with regard to the Son of David. They are divine characteristics, so that when the blind men appeal to Jesus, Son of David, to have mercy on them, it is because they recognize Jesus as the true king about whom the Lord himself said in Psalm 2, "You are my son, today I have begotten you" (Ps 2:7), and who in Psalm 72 "rescues the poor when they cry out, the oppressed who have no one to help. . . . shows pity to the needy . . . and saves the lives of the poor" (Ps 72:12, 13).

The cry "Have mercy" and the invocation "Son of David" run through the gospel of Matthew from beginning to end like a refrain to a psalm, as if the entire gospel were one great antiphonal liturgy.

This very encounter between Jesus and two blind men is itself like a refrain in Matthew's text; it is repeated at the very end of chapter twenty. There, too, the two men cry out, "Have mercy on us, Son of David." Jesus asks what they want, and they respond, "Lord, let our eyes be opened." In pity, Jesus touches their eyes, and immediately they see—and follow him (Matt 20:29-34). Then immediately comes the triumphal entry into Jerusalem, where the crowd going before and after him cry out, "Hosanna to the Son of David," and add, "this is the prophet Jesus from Nazareth in Galilee" (Matt 21:1-10).

The two blind men in chapter twenty followed Jesus after their eyes were opened. The two in chapter nine, by contrast, follow him before their eyes are opened, follow him even into the house.

We might wonder how blind men might follow Jesus, but then we only have to look at ourselves. We follow Jesus; we have followed him right into his house, this monastery, and which of us does not cry out at one time or another, "Have mercy on us, Son of David"? Indeed, we make that cry several times every day, especially at the beginning of Mass.

And there is something liturgical about this story of the two blind men in chapter nine of Matthew, something of a baptismal rite with catechesis and missioning. The two blind men who follow Jesus are catechumens. They follow him into the house, where they receive interrogation about their faith, just as neophytes still do at the Easter Vigil. And we, how many significant times in our monastic life have we not stood before the superior and in front of witnesses and been interrogated, "What do you seek?" "The Mercy of God," we reply each time.

The interrogation: "Do you believe I am able to do this?"

The response of faith: "Yes, Lord."

Then comes the baptismal illumination, when with word and gesture Jesus opens their eyes.

We know that in the early church neophytes were not to tell outsiders what happened "in the house." So here, Jesus says, "See that no one knows it."

"See," he says. His characteristic playful irony, inherited from his mother, signals to the formerly sightless neophytes that he does not intend them to take him seriously.

And in fact the neophytes now illumined become really mature disciples, truly following him by disobeying, going away, and spreading his fame in that entire land.

I think of us, our questions about our future. None of the blind men was content to remain as he was, or to stay where he was. Those of the first set followed Jesus into the house, however improbable it is to imagine blind people following someone that way, and those of the second set cried out, even as the sensible crowd tried to silence them, "Son of David, have mercy on us!"

Obvious and irreversible disadvantage is no reason to keep settling for the necessary when the impossible is just on the other side of the possible. It no doubt took something for both sets to move and act in ways different from what was reasonable and even safe. That something was the new wine whose aroma they sensed as Jesus passed them. Questions like "How can we keep doing what we are doing?" and "How can we survive?" (without making a move) are not Gospel questions; they are not monastic questions. They are materialists' questions, shortsighted, because nothing stays the same, and survival is a dream in the night of the fear of death.

They are questions that do not merit even the question "Do you believe that I am able to do this?"

For the Gospel is not about maintaining but about conversion, not surviving but death in the hope of resurrection, which is entirely grace and the newness of God. The Holy Spirit is hope. Saint Bernard writes, "It is scarcely possible to avoid doubts about the truth when we lack the light of the Holy Spirit; but it is another thing to hanker after erroneous opinions. . . .When this Spirit is silent we must be alert and hold falsehood in abhorrence, even if bound in the clutches of perplexing incertitude . . . [rather than] pursue with disastrous assurance an erroneous course of our own" (SC 17.3; CF 4:128).

44

On Matthew 9:32-37

(Mark 2:12; 3:22; 4:23; 6:34; 7:37;
Luke 8:1; 11:14-15)

Our commentary on the gospel of Matthew has brought us to the end of chapter nine. In chapters eight and nine Jesus cleansed a leper, healed a centurion's child, raised up Peter's mother-in-law, calmed a storm at sea, cast out the demons from the men of Gadara, healed a paralytic, raised a ruler's daughter to life, healed a woman with a hemorrhage, and, finally, restored sight to two blind men.

We call these acts of Jesus miracles, and there are many of them. Mark records eighteen miracles, and Matthew and Luke together record ten additional ones. John calls them *signs* and records seven signs peculiar to his gospel. Whatever else we can say about Jesus in the gospels, it is clear that he is a miracle worker. He is a teacher, but, like sacraments, his words are accompanied by deeds.

Before Matthew closes chapter nine he records another miracle. Jesus has just cured two blind men. Then, "As they were going, behold, a dumb demoniac was brought to him" (Matt 9:32). Matthew links the two miracles with the phrase "as they were going."

But for some reason Matthew is almost shy about this last miracle, maybe embarrassed, certainly reticent and vague in describing it. In fact, he does not describe the miracle at all, but only its results: "And when the demon had been cast out, the dumb man spoke" (Matt 9:33).

There is no contact between Jesus and the dumb man. We assume that it was Jesus who cast out the demon, but Matthew does not say. It is all by association and implication, and yet the response of the crowds is anything but ambiguous: they "marveled, saying, 'Never was anything like this seen in Israel'" (Matt 9:33).

And, we can say, never was anything like this seen anywhere else in the known world. There were miracles and miracle workers for sure. Think of Elijah and Elisha in the Books of Kings. But not *like this*, as the crowd put it. In performing his miracles, Jesus never invoked a name, not even the name of God; he acted on his own authority. He never used magic or staged a situation where he could then perform a miracle to impress people.

Most important, Jesus' miracles were always for other people, never for himself. This fact holds true even for the "signs" in John's gospel.

You might argue that the signs were for the purpose of manifesting Jesus as Son of God, for authenticating Jesus. Rather, they were at one and the same time gifts for people truly in need and, as Jesus says about the raising of Lazarus, "that you may believe" (John 11:15), one of the Good Things that are gifts of the Father (see #28). Jesus was never taken in by the temptation, "What sign can you do, that we may see and believe in you?" (John 6:30).

On this solemnity of the Epiphany of the Lord, we are moved to see Jesus' miracles and signs as epiphanies. In John the signs manifest Jesus' glory, his divine nature; in Matthew, Mark, and Luke, they manifest the presence in loving Jesus of the kingdom of God. But these are two ways of saying the same thing.

The glory of God incarnate and living among us in Jesus of Nazareth and in the church's sacraments *is* the nearness of the kingdom of God, the kingdom of God among you.

Jesus, in fact, summed up his entire aim in terms not of words but of exorcisms and cures, signs and miracles: "Behold, I cast out demons, and I perform healings today, and tomorrow, and on the third day I accomplish my purpose" (Luke 13:32).

Matthew ends chapter nine looking back and pointing ahead: "And Jesus went about . . . teaching . . . and preaching the gospel of the kingdom, and healing every disease and every infirmity. . . . Then he said to his disciples, . . . 'pray therefore'" for laborers for the harvest (Matt 9:35-38).

Then, hardly does chapter ten start when Jesus says to the Twelve, "preach as you go, 'the kingdom of heaven is at hand,' Heal the sick, raise the dead, cleanse lepers, cast out demons."

Following Jesus, the church's mission is an eschatological epiphany of the glory of God in works of mercy, eliciting faith and imparting joy. At the end of Mass the deacon or priest says, "Go, and announce the gospel of the Lord." "You received without pay, give without pay" (Matt 10:7-8).

> *I have not forsaken you.*
> Did I say you had forsaken me?
> *No, but you'll beg the question.*
> So, will you?
> *Call me by your name.*
> Jesus?
> *Emmanuel.*